Fernand Léger: CONTRASTS OF FORMS

Matthew Affron

with an essay by Maria Gough

UNIVERSITY OF VIRGINIA ART MUSEUM

CHARLOTTESVILLE

This book was published on the occasion of the exhibition
Fernand Léger: Contrasts of Forms

University of Virginia Art Museum
January 19–March 18, 2007

Fogg Art Museum
Harvard University Art Museums
April 14–June 10, 2007

Published by the University of Virginia Art Museum
www.virginia.edu/artmuseum

Distributed by The Pennsylvania State University Press

Printed with private funds provided by the Oakwood Foundation

ISBN: 0-9706263-3-9

Designer: Diane Nelson
Printer: Peake DeLancey Printers

Cover illustration:
catalogue no. 4
Fernand Léger
Composition (Contrast of Forms)
1912–13
Gouache, brush, and India ink on buff paper, mounted on board
23½ x 20 in., (59.6 x 50.8 cm.)
Collection Michael and Judy Steinhardt, New York

Foreword

JILL HARTZ, DIRECTOR

The exhibition *Fernand Léger: Contrasts of Forms* and this accompanying publication go to the heart of the mission of the University of Virginia Art Museum—to serve diverse audiences through innovative models of learning based in the visual arts. With this project we strive to share with students of all ages our appreciation of one of the most renowned artists of the twentieth century and, in doing so, to foster new educational experiences.

A few years ago, the University created an academic post for Matthew Affron, already a faculty member of the McIntire Department of Art. As Director of Special Curatorial Projects, Mr. Affron became a liaison between the Museum and the University's academic departments and an initiator of projects aimed at bringing the visual arts into core teaching areas, from art and architecture to English, history, religious studies, and more. The present exhibition is exemplary in this regard, as Mr. Affron is himself a teacher and a specialist in the work of Léger.

Under the direction of Mr. Affron, we are pleased to present a special exhibition that exclusively explores Léger's *Contrasts of Forms* series. Although this body of works has received consideration by other art historians, there is a great deal more that can be understood about the artist and his time by looking closely at this singular group of works on paper and canvas. I am indebted to Mr. Affron for curating this illuminating show and for his major contribution to the catalogue and to Maria Gough for her stimulating essay.

Following its presentation in Charlottesville, this exhibition will travel to the Fogg Art Meseum, one of the esteemed Harvard University Museums in Cambridge, Massachusetts, where it will be on view April 14 through June 10, 2007. For their efforts in bringing the exhibition to the Fogg, I thank Thomas W. Lentz, Elizabeth and John Moors Cabot Director; Harry Cooper, Curator of Modern Art; Maureen Donovan, Director of Collections Management; and Danielle Hanrahan, Head of Exhibition Design and Installation. The presentation of *Fernand Léger: Contrasts of Forms* at Harvard is supported by The Alexander S., Robert L., and Bruce A. Beal Exhibition Fund.

Mounting even a small exhibition of work by such an internationally acclaimed artist takes considerable resources. For the loans of their work, I thank Judy and Michael Steinhardt and the other private collectors, The Alex Hillman Family Foundation, the Albright-Knox Art Gallery, The Solomon R. Guggenheim Museum, The Metropolitan Museum of Art, and The Museum of Modern Art. The exhibition is made possible with the generous support of The Eugene V. and Clare E. Thaw Charitable Trust, the University of Virginia Art Museum Volunteer Board, the Office of the Dean of the College of Arts & Sciences and the Carl H. and Martha S. Lindner Center for Art History at the University of Virginia, an anonymous gift, Nicholas Acquavella, Sheila and Ted Weschler, and Sheridan W. and Thomas F. Nicholson. For this handsome publication, I am deeply indebted to the Oakwood Foundation.

Acknowledgments

I am very grateful to the collectors who lent to the exhibition and to the many colleagues who facilitated the loans that were made by their museums.

I thank my colleagues at the University of Virginia Art Museum who contributed to every phase of work for this exhibition: Jill Hartz, director; Andrea Douglas, curator of collections and exhibitions; Jean Lancaster Collier, collections manager; Claire Holman Thompson, director of development; David Chennault, associate director of administration; Diana Snead, accounting specialist; and Anamarie Liddell, preparator.

I thank Maria Gough for the excellent essay she contributed to the catalogue.

I am indebted to Harry Cooper, Curator of Modern Art at the Fogg Art Museum, for his generous collaboration and contributions to this project.

For the expertise and advice they offered at many stages of the project, I express special appreciation to Nicholas Acquavella, Emily Braun, and Jodi Hauptman. Marjorie Shelley and Rachel Mustalish of The Metropolitan Museum of Art provided invaluable information on the topic of Léger's drawing materials and technique. Brigitte Hedel-Samson and Nelly Maillard of the Musée National Fernand Léger answered many questions. Lucy Rosenfeld kindly read my essay, and I thank her for her editorial suggestions. I am very happy to acknowledge colleagues, friends, and family who provided support and guidance: Charles and Mirella Affron, Paul Barolsky, Lee White Galvis, Franck Giraud, Larry Goedde, Mitchell Merling, Charles Moffett, David Nash, David Summers, Kenneth Wayne, and Jeffrey Weiss. I would like to thank my teacher, Robert Herbert. As always, my deepest debts are to Sophie Rosenfeld.

MATTHEW AFFRON

Director of Special Curatorial Projects
Associate Professor of Art
University of Virginia

Léger's Law of Contrasts

MATTHEW AFFRON

Over the course of two years, between 1912 and 1914, Fernand Léger developed a remarkable cycle of images comprising some fifty canvases and perhaps twice as many related works on paper. This series is known today under the rubric *Contrasts of Forms*. The cycle encompasses a wide variety of traditional and brashly modernist subjects, including still lifes, figure studies, and landscapes of village and city. But its core is a set of compositions, which, like *Composition (Contrast of Forms)* (1912–13, cat. 4), sweep aside representational themes and replace them with an abstract motif. It is Léger's distinctive way of handling visual form that justifies thinking of all these works as a coherent group. The *Contrasts* are set apart by a complex visual vocabulary consisting of geometric stylizations—cones, sections of cylinders, drums, cubes, and planes—all sharply outlined and scrubbed with patches of saturated color (in the canvases) or stark white and black (in the works on paper).

The *Contrasts* have long been recognized as essential to two great chapters in the history of modern art in the years before the First World War: first, the development of cubism, and second, the emergence of abstract art. Moreover, they cap the initial, pre-1914 phase of Léger's career when, as the critic and curator Douglas Cooper wrote in the catalogue for a 1962 show devoted to these compositions, the artist finds his signature pictorial maneuvers and, in effect, becomes Léger.[1]

The exhibition *Fernand Léger: Contrasts of Forms* tells the story of this cycle in twelve examples. These include a charcoal sketch, ten very fully developed compositions in ink, gouache, and oil, and one major canvas. The selection of works covers the series' chronological arc and extends to nearly the full range of motifs that appear in it. This exhibition makes it possible to consider closely the development of Léger's handling of form and theme. It also affords an opportunity to examine the ways in which Léger worked on canvas and on paper, a comparison that is essential for understanding the *Contrasts of Forms* idea. The present essay examines the logic of Léger's *Contrasts* and the importance of this cycle in shaping the character of his art.

Contrasts of Forms

With the oil and gouache *Study for "Nude Model in the Studio"/Composition I* (1912, cat. 2), we find Léger at a moment of transition. An artist's model takes a standard pose with her right arm stretched overhead. The body is created from segments of ovals, modeled in light and dark, which clash against one another and against the mostly angular surround of the studio interior. "Léger enjoys expressing the round forms of a nude woman in a rectilinear studio," offered the critic André Warnod in his review of the opening of the Salon des Indépendants in March 1913.[2] He must have been describing this or one of the other studies for Léger's *Nude Model in the Studio* (1913, Solomon R. Guggenheim Museum, New York), for only those studies on paper were ready for viewing at the opening of the exhibition. They were joined later by the definitive version in oil.

Warnod's remark points out one of the most conspicuous attributes of Léger's image of the nude model: the element of formal severity. In a cubist context, this signified an interest in stripping the language of art to its essentials and an effort to rethink the manner in which bodies and spaces might be represented. Warnod's comment only hints, though, at another conspicuous feature, the stress on visual patterns that seem to push subject matter to the brink of occultation. But this, too, was a constant theme of Léger's work during this period. Consider the charcoal drawing *Contrast of Forms* (1912, cat. 3). One side of the sheet presents a study of the model against a neutral background, arms and legs churning in counterclockwise rotation. On the other side, the woman's forms are reduced to less anatomically specific, more all-purpose units, mainly broken circles and ovals, against a field of sharp planes. This basic arrangement of lines and forms, in addition to being highly abstracted, is endowed with great visual flexibility; it conveys the image of a nude model here, but works very differently elsewhere. Compare a study on another of Léger's favorite themes, the view out the studio window and onto the city. In *Smoke over the Rooftops* (1912, cat. 1), the interlocked semicircles represent rising puffs of smoke against the rectangular buildings in Paris.

When was the "first" of the *Contrasts*? Because the cycle is so directly rooted in the works of the preceding few years, there has never been a clear-cut answer to this question. And yet, the cycle stands on its own. This can be explained in terms of both an internal stylistic dynamic and by factors that framed the production of the work. Starting in the autumn of 1910, Léger had traveled in a circle of painters who found success by scandal at such venues as the more liberal annual Salons—the springtime Indépendants and its end-of-year counterpart, the Salon d'Automne. To be noticed in such venues meant painting large canvases for high visibility. Léger followed this pattern even though the fading of substantial subject matter in his work soon became an issue much discussed by exhibition reviewers. But by late 1912 or early 1913, Daniel-Henry Kahnweiler, the dealer who played an instrumental role in promoting avant-garde art in Paris, had taken an interest in work. He purchased all of the paintings in the artist's possession, and a monopoly contract was signed in October 1913. This put Léger in the exclusive circle of Galerie Kahnweiler cubists. Following the gallery's protocol, he withdrew from exhibiting new work at the salons and in other venues in Paris. This change came together with a shift in the rhythm and direction of Léger's work. Now, instead of working in very large formats he proceeded in a more open-ended and continuous way, in relatively smaller canvases and with an increased rate of production. The result was the *Contrasts*, a two-year effort that came to an abrupt close with the outbreak of war in the summer of 1914.

To define the methodology of the *Contrasts*, it is most helpful to begin with the works on paper. Léger used a variety of dry and water-based media during these years, but the essence of his style is best captured in the most substantial and highly embellished drawings, works of the type included in the present exhibition. These drawings were executed with a brush in various combinations of ink, gouache, and oil paint. The paper is smooth and allows the drawing of contours with thin, continuous strokes. Intense lights and deep shadows are filled in with vigorous brushwork that is alternately wet and dry, shiny and matte, impastoed and smooth. Early in the cycle, Léger's forms are mainly planar and frontal, like the broken circles and quadrilaterals of the *Study for "Nude Model in the Studio."* These shapes seem to hang on a compositional scaffold, slanting this way and that to catch glimmers of light and pieces of shadow. Soon, however, Léger increases the plasticity of his forms.

With the *Contrasts of Forms*, Léger undertakes a fundamental transformation of the conventions of representation, or the techniques for depicting still lifes, figure studies, and landscapes. He concentrates on two conventions of pictorial illusionism: the construction of pictorial depth and the modeling of figures in light and dark. The effect of three dimensions is achieved by means of very simple perspective devices. In *Two Reclining Women* (1913, cat. 5), the oblique couch rails lead the eye into depth and the overlapping of the bodies of the two studio models suggests that they lie on two planes parallel to the picture plane. And yet this movement into depth turns back on itself. The compositional field, so packed full of forms, seems to build forward and outward. Use of the technique of *passage*—the breaking of the boundaries of solid forms and the sharing of contours—causes forms to merge and to seem to share corners of space without, paradoxically, destroying each other. This tendency to counter perspective illusionism is most intense in *Study for "Contrast of Forms"* (1913, cat. 6), *Contrast of Forms* (1913, cat. 7), and other compositions that present abstract motifs. Here, Léger tends to angle his building blocks along multiple axes of projection, thus generating moments of extremely dynamic structural interplay, especially at the center of the compositional field.

The handling of light and dark is the other distinctive aspect of Léger's rethinking of illusionism in the *Contrasts* drawings. The basic method is a variation on the old-master technique of chiaroscuro drawing. In chiaroscuro drawing the artist, instead of putting dark marks on a light-colored sheet, begins with toned paper and draws in contrasting light and dark strokes. Tonal values are reduced to just three. Black reads as shadow, white reads as highlight, and the paper has two functions, at once providing a middle tone for modeling three-dimensional objects and representing a minimally defined, relatively shady background, a shallow depth from which solid figures emerge into atmospheric light. Chiaroscuro drawings are typically characterized by super-refined effects of light and dark—but this clearly is quite foreign to Léger's sensibility. He reaches the opposite way, for directness, impetuousness, irreducibility, and absolute contrasts. In chiaroscuro drawing, dramatic strokes of white play off deep darks to generate the illusion of volume and relief. But those highlights also assert a power of embellishment apart from any depicted object. They produce an independent effect of sparkle. This visual dazzle is the technique's truly distinguishing trait. Léger exploits it for all it is worth.[3]

So how then are the drawings related to their counterparts on canvas? Made on loose sheets of inexpensive paper, the drawings clearly served as sketches or studies for the paintings. And yet, as is demonstrated in this exhibition, many are so substantial that they demand to be considered as works in their own right. The relationship is complicated in a further and much deeper way when we consider a very important difference in the way Léger works on paper as compared with canvas. The world of these drawings is chromatically limited: black, white, and the dark off-white of the paper. The paintings, on the other hand, are highly colored. In other words, Léger did not simply transpose his blunt, irreducible three-tone drawing technique to canvas. Rather, he explored parallel intentions with different means.[4]

Contrast of Forms (1913, cat. 13) and other paintings display sharply outlined forms and rough, open brushwork. Pigment rarely comes all the way to the edges of those depicted forms, so an off-white preparatory layer shows through, both within their borders and in the spaces between them. This accentuated lack of finish fights against the illusion of three-dimensional plasticity, and it calls attention to the materiality of the medium. Léger piles his building blocks irregularly, in a polycentric space. While all of this is similar to the drawings, the canvases establish their own direction by his dramatic use of color. Some of the paintings use a palette that is restricted to brilliant white, black, and the three pigment primaries of red, yellow, and blue. Others add intensely saturated oranges, yellows, greens, and violets in different combinations. In all of the canvases, color swallows traditional chiaroscuro. Sharp hues take over as the element that most determines the visibility of what is presented. They simplify and amplify both shape and form, introducing an aspect of clarity amid the ambiguity of tumbling shapes. In the 1914 landscape *Village in the Forest* (cat. 12), for example, areas of red, blue, and green serve to separate the planes of the cubic houses and to set one building apart from the next. There are also localized instances of modeling in color, where colors of different light and dark values appear on adjacent surfaces of a single form and indicate the protrusion of that form from the background.

For Léger, the concreteness of the object and its abstraction go hand in hand. It is evident at a glance that the solidity of the houses in his landscapes, or the integrity of the objects on tables or of the forms of human bodies, is perpetually under pressure from a countervailing tendency toward flatness, breakup, and abstraction. This conflict is encoded within Léger's color system. Thus, while colors in these paintings do sometimes reasonably approximate the actual hue of represented things, like the green of the trees in *Village in the Forest*, this type of correspondence is quickly cancelled as adjacent colors stray from real-world hues, appearing as absolute and independent from any reference to landscape. In terms of his overall color strategy, Léger selected colors that would be, he believed, extremely dissonant and self-isolating when juxtaposed. Even in the paintings with discernable subject matter, such as *Village in the Forest*, the ensemble of light and dark values and polychromy is conceived as an organized totality. It constructs a visual motif—what is called the *coloris* in French.

And what of Léger's whites? They provide information about the shape and texture of objects, and the direction of the represented light that hits them. One face of a cubic object or of a step-form will display a strong local color, which we take to be an inherent quality of it, while the color of an adjacent face of the same form will be washed out by light. A slightly more gradual shift from intense local color to bright light on a single plane, on the other hand, suggests the angling of that plane relative to the light source. This is modeling of an extremely brutal and direct type. It constructs the effect of tangible form, but it also abstracts the image.

Léger is looking for a new language of light, an intensity, concentration, and mobility of light beyond the limits of naturalism. Some of the most intense incidents of light in these works are those that fall on the most steeply curved surfaces, such as the drum-shaped forms in *Study for "Still Life"* and *Study for the Painting "Still Life with Alarm Clock"* (1913 and 1914; cats. 8 and 11), the bulbous poplars in *Village in the Forest* and other landscapes, and the tubular limbs of the humanoids in the figure studies: the reclining nudes, women in interiors, and figures on staircases and balconies in outdoor urban settings. Léger runs strips of highlight up and down the length of these rounded, arched forms. He brackets that central highlight with two darker tones, black in the drawings, as in the studies for *The Staircase* (1913; cats. 9 and 10), and colors in the equivalent canvases (a striking example is *The Staircase*, 1913, Kunsthaus, Zurich). These bracketed ridges of highlight make curved forms stand out. But they also set up a very special optical effect, the extraordinarily bright and highly charged type of light reflection that is called luster. In both Léger's drawings and his paintings, brilliant, unpredictable, dynamic luster is the essence of a shift from pictorial illusionism to abstraction.[5]

It is, of course, a modernist truism that artistic conventions must change and the new must sweep away the old. The *Contrasts* detach graphic marks, composition, value contrasts, and color from their traditional representational tasks and put them toward new pictorial inventions. The classic and still most authoritative analysis of this process as it pertains to the *Contrasts* is the first piece of writing ever published on these works, a chapter in Kahnweiler's book *The Rise of Cubism*, published in 1920. The role of the writer on art was a new one for the dealer, for he had previously avoided public commentary on the artists he supported, believing that his sector of the art market separated from the larger art world and its noisy public debates and that enlightened artists and amateurs needed to operate in a more protected sphere.[6] But the war had forced him, as a German national, to close his business. He emigrated to Bern in the summer of 1914 and occupied himself in studying philosophy at the local university and writing about the artists who interested him. *The Rise of Cubism* is Kahnweiler's narrative of pre-war cubism through the work of three painters whom he had backed in earlier days, Pablo Picasso, Georges Braque, and Fernand Léger. A distinctive critical physiognomy emerges in this and other early writings. Borrowing his key terms from neo-Kantian philosophy, Kahnweiler defines cubism as a system of painterly signs that stand for and reveal the mind's objective ordering of sensory experience. These views would make a strong mark on literature about cubism, from Alfred Barr's exhibition catalogue of 1936, *Cubism and Abstract Art*, to recent structuralist and deconstructionist interpretations.[7]

Kahnweiler does not present a survey of Léger's prewar art in *The Rise of Cubism*.[8] He touches on *Nudes in the Forest* (Kröller-Müller Museum, Otterlo, 1909-10), the austere and tumultuous update of the neoclassical composed landscape that marked Léger's emergence as a central figure within the burgeoning cubist group, and he alludes to the intensification of the power of color in the pictures that followed. But then he moves straight to the matter at hand, a discussion of the *Contrasts* as part of the cubist story. "We have recognized Cubism," Kahnweiler asserts, "as the endeavor to capture the three dimensional diversity of the outer world within the unity of the painting." For Kahnweiler, in other words, Léger, like the other cubist painters, begins with formal simplification and a search for beauty in the elemental. His distinctiveness rests upon the means used to attain this end. Kahnweiler points out, first, Léger's extremely "arbitrary" handling of represented objects and the lengths to which he is willing to go toward the suppression of any and all representational links to specific things in the world. Kahnweiler labors and hesitates over this point, stressing that Léger's work is not abstract in what the critic understands to be the negative sense of the term (meaning mere decoration or surface adornment), but rather that it is deeply structural and powerfully material. Léger, says Kahnweiler, is an artist who distills motifs to their underlying geometries and discovers in that geometrical framework the reality beneath appearances.

Kahnweiler's second observation about Léger's distinct contribution to cubism follows directly from the first—it concerns Léger's use of color as a pictorial device. "An artist who treats the forms of the object so outrageously certainly cannot regard its color as inviolable; that is understandable. He colors the forms in his paintings arbitrarily, in accordance with their function in the work."[9] The importance of the notion of "arbitrary" forms and colors is underscored here by the repeated use of the word. Roughly speaking, it means at the discretion and judgment of the artist, and not tied to subject matter by the logic of resemblance. The notion of "arbitrary" colors had some currency in the days of the impressionists and the post-impressionists, when it expressed the idea that color could be the basis of a new kind of idealistic and abstract art. Kahweiler uses the idea to say that new form begets new color, and vice versa. He underscores the idea in closing his chapter with a vivid description of Léger's tumultuous, dynamic style. "And now, what does Léger really want? He wants to produce an effect. He strives for the weightiest three-dimensionality of form and for stridency of color. He is animated by a desire to endow his painting with power, to make it dominate and sweep everything before it. Léger's work shows a wealth of unspent, boundlessly seething strength."[10]

The Law of Contrasts

"Contrast" is a key word for the interpretation of Léger's art. This word has a singular frequency of use, flexibility and breadth of implication, and conceptual resonance within the large body of writings that the artist produced in the course of his career. "Contrast" is an idea that produced an aesthetic. It stands for something like a world view. And it was first defined in two famous lectures that coincided in time with the *Contrasts* cycle. Léger delivered these lectures in May 1913 and May 1914 at the Académie Wassilieff, an informal drawing academy and meeting place for the bohemian and cosmopolitan circles of Montparnasse, then the hub of avant-garde Paris. The lectures were quickly published in small avant-garde periodicals in Paris and overseas.

In the Wassilieff lectures, "contrast" is first of all Léger's label for a method of painting based on stark distinctions: oppositions of value, line, and color, of curved and straight lines, of flat surfaces against modeled ones. This would be a durable principle. Léger would continue speaking until very late in life of a "law of plastic contrasts" as the basis of his work. "I apply the law of plastic contrasts," he wrote in a typical comment of 1923. "I group contrary values together; flat surfaces opposed to modeled surfaces; volumetric figures opposed to the flat façades of houses; molded volumes of plumes of smoke to active surfaces of architecture; pure, flat tones opposed to gray, modulated tones or the reverse."[11] Yet, from the first, "contrast" also had a much wider scope, as Léger's word for the distinctive visual experiences of modern life, experiences that he believed profoundly shape the way modern people see, feel, think, and produce symbolic forms such as paintings. Finally, these considerations on "contrast" as the principle of mediation between modern art and modern life led Léger directly to a set of arguments about the social tasks and goals of art.

The first Wassilieff lecture begins and ends with reflections on the theme of illusionism and anti-illusionism in the visual arts. The modern is a turning point, says Léger. Traditional forms of painting were based in the rule of likeness to nature and for that reason provided only superficial visual satisfaction. They were overthrown by forms of painting that concentrate on the means of pictorial expression themselves. The work of art is an organized arrangement of abstract pictorial signs, and true expression and real invention are grounded in the non-mimetic elements of the image. Léger defends these ideas by invoking figures of authority from the history of nineteenth-century French painting. He follows a standard narrative in tracing the transformation of the formal language of painting back to the bold, colorist art of Eugène Delacroix, Édouard Manet's modeling in abrupt value contrasts, and the abstraction of the image in impressionist painting. This lineage continues with Georges Seurat's optical mixture, the method of juxtaposing visually distinct touches of color in mutually intensifying relations of opposition. It is hardly surprising that this particular genealogy should be on Léger's mind. Like many other young painters of his generation he remained marked by having done his modernist apprenticeship within a post-1900 revival of neo-impressionist painting. Léger's interest in pure color as pictorial

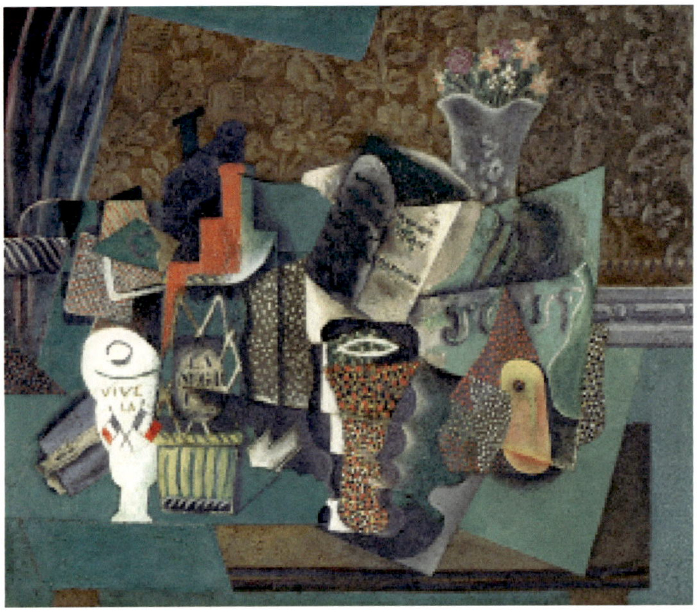

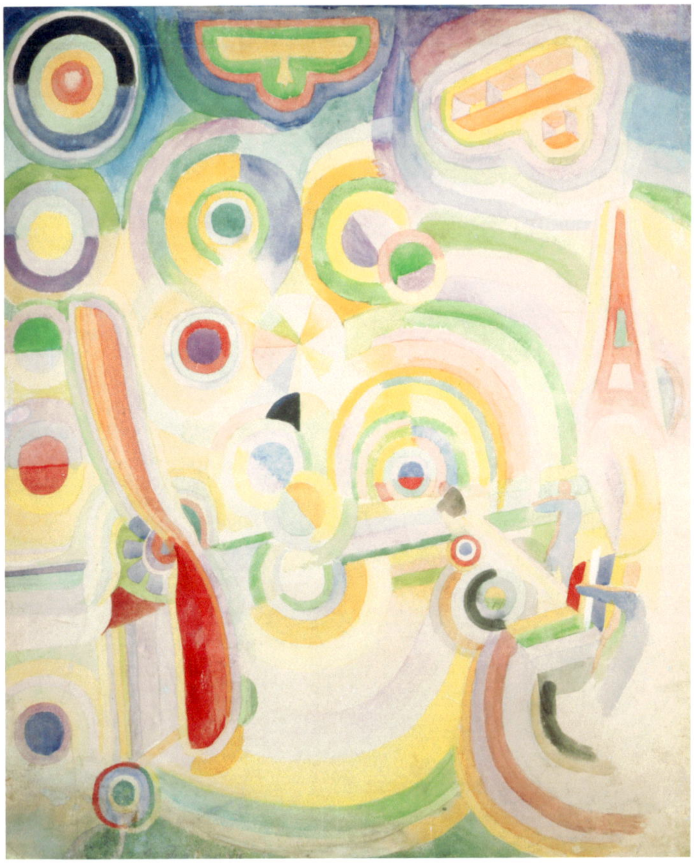

Figure 1. (above) Pablo Picasso. *Still Life with Cards, Glasses, and Bottle of Rum: Vive la France,* 1914. Oil and sand on canvas, 21 3/8 x 25 3/4 in. (54.2 x 65.4 cm.). Private Collection. Photograph © Dorothy Zeidman

Figure 2. Robert Delaunay. *Hommage à Blériot*, ca. 1913–14 Watercolor on paper, 30 7/10 x 26 2/5 in. (78 x 67 cm.) Musee d'Art Moderne de la Ville de Paris, Paris, France Photo: Giraudon/Art Resource, NY

raw material and his conception of this color as a liberating force in art still connected him to that model in 1913 and 1914.

The true hero of Léger's story, however, is Paul Cézanne, who took up the impressionist transformation of conventional chiaroscuro and built it into an integrated system of line, form, and color.[12] The first Wassilieff lecture features extensive paraphrase and direct quotations from an influential interpretive essay by the painter-critic Émile Bernard, which had recently been reissued in book form following its initial publication in 1904. Léger follows Bernard in speaking of Cézanne as the inventor of a solidly structured and optically energetic manner of painting. A non-standard published version of Léger's lecture (it appeared in the German periodical *Der Sturm* in August 1913) paraphrases Cézanne's famous recommendation, reported by Bernard, that the painter interpret nature's forms as abstract geometrical entities, that is, the sphere, the cylinder, and the cone, arranged in multiple systems of projection and endowed with an ever-shifting, structure-altering coloration.[13] Cézanne's lesson, as Léger construed it, was simply this: "Pictorial contrasts used in their purest sense (complementary colors, lines, and forms) are henceforth the structural basis of modern pictures."[14]

Léger was convinced that contemporary achievements in painting would necessarily carry forward impressionist and post-impressionist achievements. His reflections on this aesthetic heritage thus also served as a way to talk about the current state of things and to establish his standpoint in relation to friends and rivals in the larger field of cubist discourse. The two most relevant comparisons are in the work of Picasso and Robert Delaunay. Picasso's *Still Life with Cards, Glasses, and Bottle of Rum: Vive la France* (private collection, 1914, fig. 1) centers on a wineglass covered with brilliant points of color to represent stippled light playing upon it. These points of color are a clear nod to Seurat, but they are part of a larger and intentionally mixed scheme: a setting that reflects and parodies the typical taste of the French domestic interior. As is typical of Picasso's cubist painting after 1912, when positive color becomes an important factor, even when color is at its most forceful and lyrical, its artificial and conventional side is always emphasized.

Thus, in this example, Seurat's influence is made to compete with the painted wallpaper pattern, the flowers, and the blue, white, and red of the French tricolors. Those crossed flags adorn the cutout form of a white glass, but because they are made to overlap the adjacent bottle of rum, they also appear as an ornament applied to the picture surface itself. In this sense they are not unlike the flat paper planes of Picasso's *papiers collés*.[15] Léger was not sympathetic to this way of composing pictures, and he stressed this difference in a letter he wrote to Kahnweiler in 1919, at the moment when Kahnweiler was preparing to write the Léger chapter in *The Rise of Cubism*. "[I use] volumes in movement tinted in local colors, and to accentuate the movement, oppositions of contrasts."[16]

Léger was also disinclined toward the methods of his friend Delaunay, but for different reasons. Delaunay began with a vitalistic conception of color: color as pure energy, equivalent to the light of the sun and extending across natural and artificial spectrums, which energizes the eye and carries it to new heights of experience. A watercolor study (ca. 1913–14, Musée d'Art Moderne de la Ville de Paris, fig. 2) for Delaunay's 1914 encomium to a French aviator, *Homage to Blériot*, is filled with circular forms that represent, variously, the rays of the sun, those rays refracted by the rotary motion of an airplane propeller (at the lower left), and the electric signals of the airfield. The circular tricolor insignia in the lower right quadrant, yet another disc, refers to Blériot's status as a national hero following his pioneering flight over the English Channel in 1909. In pictorial terms, these color-discs construct a cosmic space. In discursive terms, they are related metaphorically to the painter's color circle and to the chromatic wheel of modern color science, which Delaunay saw as the basis of a pure and universal grammar of painting, which is rooted in but surpasses what had been achieved by his impressionist and post-impressionist predecessors.[17]

Léger saw himself as engaged with Delaunay in a color quarrel. He thought that Delaunay, in constructing exclusively through color vibration, produced results that were too homogeneous and too impalpably optical, and he made this one of the major polemical themes of both Wassilieff lectures. Delaunay would retort in a notebook entry of the early 1930s, saying that "color is born of neither modeling nor of chiaroscuro; color is the only true drawing. There is no drawing with color put over top, as with Léger, as with Cormon."[18] The invocation of the name of Fernand Cormon, the Beaux-Arts master whose studio Léger had frequented for a time during his student days, served to imply that Léger's technique actually marked a regression to old-fashioned painterly decorums (Delaunay also remembered squabbling over art matters with his uncle, a traditionalist painter who also had been a student of Cormon).[19] Whatever we might make of the rhetoric, this disagreement underlined an important difference of approach, which can be demonstrated with Léger's *The Fourteenth of July* (1914, Musée National Fernand Léger, Biot, fig. 3), a tricolor-themed picture made only weeks prior to the declaration of war and Léger's military mobilization. *The Fourteenth of July* uses the basic *Contrasts* scheme: strong outlines, flattened and sculptural form-elements, heavy brushstrokes, brilliant red, white, blue, green, and yellow. It is highly unusual within the cycle in taking up a topical and commemorative theme.

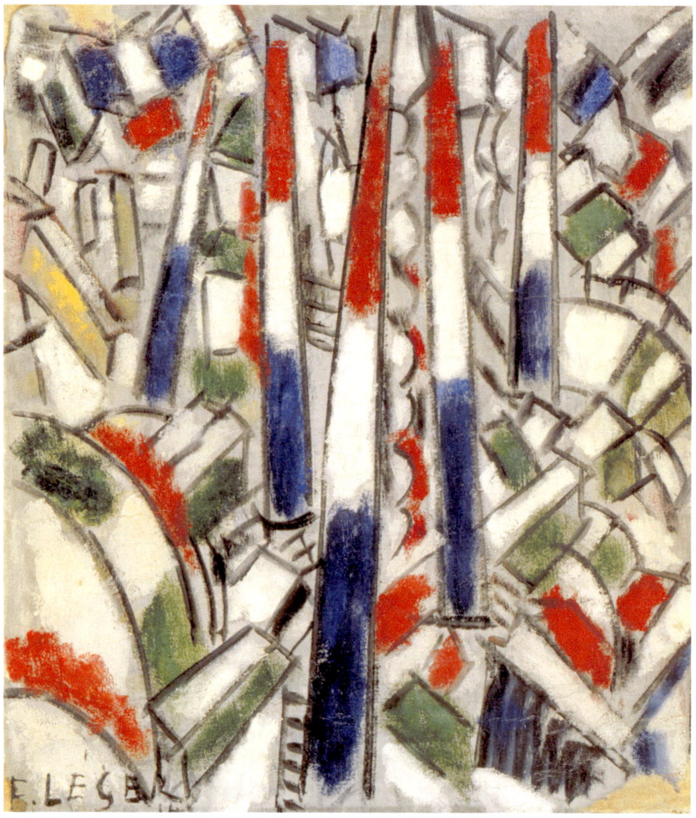

Figure 3. Fernand Léger. *The Fourteenth of July,* 1914. Oil on canvas, 25⅘ x 23 in. (65.5 x 58.5 cm.). Musée National Fernand Léger, Biot, France. *Photo: Gerard Blot. Réunion des Musées Nationaux/Art Resource, NY*

The picture depicts the decor of public celebration on the national holiday of Bastille Day—a vista, perhaps a townscape, structured around the elementary rhythms of slanted tubular elements that represent trees banded blue, white, and red. The flag was ready-made for Léger's way of picturing. Its colors zip five times toward the top edge. They inject not only an extreme contrast of hue directly into the landscape but also layers of visual, expressive, and symbolic meaning.

In the Wassilieff lectures, "contrast" is Léger's shorthand term for theoretical propositions borrowed from an impressionist and post-impressionist heritage (and continued in the present) referring to the progress of painting from imitation to abstraction. It is precisely by exploring its own irreducible specificity, elaborating its intrinsic laws, exploring its own kind of truth and reality that modern painting makes its break from the past. Léger calls this process "specialization." He explains: "*Specialization is a modern thing*, and pictorial art, like all other manifestations of human genius, must submit to its law; specialization is logical, for by limiting everything to its proper purpose, it enables achievements to be intensified."[20]

If the concept of "specialization" is central to Léger's sense of the nature of art, it also determines his sense of art's changing basis in modern life. The 1914 lecture begins with remarks on the visual impact of an intensely industrialized environment, rapid modes of transportation, new techniques of visual communication, and other forces and signs of modernization. Léger speaks enthusiastically of the shock produced by illuminated signs. He discusses the impact of brightly colored posters in the landscape, a sight even more galvanizing when taken in from a fast-moving vehicle. He uses these examples to support the view that the technological and economic conditions of the present create a dense, unfixed, abbreviated, dynamic way of seeing. "Contrast," the crucial term in Léger's theory of the image as an organized system of pictorial signs, becomes the name for an order of perception based in modernization's shocks and discontinuities. The principal thesis of the second Wassilieff lecture is that modern art is shaped by and establishes its mode of existence in relation to that mode of vision. "Contemporary achievements in painting are the result of the modern mentality and are closely bound up with the visual aspect of external things that are creative and necessary for the painter," Léger states at the very beginning of the lecture. "Contemporary painting is representative, in the modern sense of the word, of the new visual state imposed by the evolution of the new means of production."[21]

He uses the word "representative," but in the modern sense. Léger reasons that since traditional representational methods are utterly thwarted by visual stimuli of modern life, any painter interested in responding to those stimuli will need to find alternate visual conventions. This idea raises the question of means and ends, of subject matter and style. Modern subjects are interesting to the painter, he admits, but not necessarily any more effective than more traditional motifs; the latter have advantages precisely because, being familiar and a little worn-out, they do not get in the way of the construction of visual form. What counts, in the end, is the way motifs are interpreted visually.

Léger's exaltation of the metropolis, mechanized travel, and new communication technologies placed him at the center of a mythology of the modern that was ascendant in Parisian avant-garde circles between 1900 and the eve of the First World War. "Contrast" was akin to "simultaneity," a catchphrase used by many in his immediate and extended cultural milieu, including the cubist painter Delaunay, but also the Italian futurist painters Umberto Boccioni and Gino Severini, the poets Guillaume Apollinaire and Blaise Cendrars, and others. Léger understood "contrast," as his colleagues did "simultaneity," as the watchword of a general modernist aesthetic, based in the raising up of big city life, its products, and its culture as the epitome of a modern order of sensation, which could be explored through formal experimentation in art.[22] The connection is made in Léger's description of oversized, brightly colored advertising posters in the landscape, with their invigorating visual shocks, as the totems of the new culture of industrialization. But these remarks had another purpose as well: to make a statement in relation to contemporary debates on the social basis of avant-garde art. The point emerges early in the 1914 lecture where Léger describes advertising posters as exemplary irritants of establishment sensibilities. "The advertising billboard, dictated by modern commercial needs, that brutally cuts across the landscape is one of the things that most infuriated so-called men of . . . good taste." He continues:

> The so-called men of good taste, the cultivated people, have never been able to stomach contrast. There is nothing worse than habit, and you will find the same people who protest with conviction in front of the billboard writing with laughter at the Salon des Indépendants in front of modern pictures, which they are incapable of swallowing. And yet, this yellow or red poster, shouting in a timid landscape, is the best of possible reasons for the new painting.[23]

Léger is thinking of an ethic of color. "Contrast," in addition to its other meanings, appears here as a social metaphor. [24] To underline the point he introduces a distinction, which had precedents in avant-gardist discourse of earlier decades, between a contemptible bourgeois tranquility and an admirable plebeian taste for strong color. "Everywhere they go the bourgeois drag their rules and their monotonous taste along with them. The peasant resists this tranquilizing sensibility, for he has retained a taste for violent contrasts in his costume, and a poster in his field does not upset him." Léger restates the point by switching the frame of reference from landscape to home, from the visual shock of the modern landscape to the static quietude of the provincial middle-class interior. "The average bourgeois has retained his ideas of tone on tone, the decorative concept. The red parlor, the yellow bedroom, will, especially in the provinces, continue to be the last word in good form for a long time. . . . This milieu is the last one an artist should frequent; truth is shrouded and feared; all that remains is manners, from which an artist can seek in vain to learn something."[25]

Public debate on cubism was frequently couched as a conflict of cultures: on the one side the members of a middlebrow public who yearned for the security of consecrated values, on the other side groups of intransigent avant-garde artists who busied themselves in knocking those same values off their pedestal. This representation of audience and artists' behavior was a well-worn scheme by the time Léger picked it up in 1914. But his rendition of it did have a specific weight because it drew on particular moments in his experience as a figure in the Parisian avant-garde. In the first place, large-scale advertising posters, so brightly colored, so full of the imagery of industry and consumerism, had for several years been a hobby horse of cultural conservatives who saw them as a sign of cultural degeneration. A legislator named Beauquier took over the presidency of a group called the Society for the Protection of the Landscape and fulminated against modern publicity as a degenerate, multicolored stain creeping over the land. The same legislator spoke out from the floor of the Chamber of Deputies against cubism as an expression of filth.[26] Léger meant to answer such arguments head-on. Second, Léger's reflections on the ethos of the middle-class interior had a direct basis in a cubist project of the fall of 1912. The furniture designer André Mare, a childhood friend of Léger's, had organized a suite of decorated rooms, called the Maison Cubiste, for the applied arts section at the Salon d'Automne, and Léger was one of the several cubist painters who he asked to contributed a canvas for display within it. Léger made a bluntly anti-decorative statement in selecting as his contribution to the display's drawing room, called the Salon Bourgeois, his picture entitled *Railroad Crossing* (1912, Fondation Beyeler, Basel), which presents the piercingly and aggressively modernist motif of a steam-belching train engine in a landscape crossed by telegraph poles.[27]

Even Léger's reflections on illusionism and anti-illusionism, the crux of the argument in the first Wassilieff lecture, were a direct response to the larger dynamic of art world controversy. In October 1912 *L'Éclair*, a Parisian daily, stoked public outrage about cubism (its difficulty, apparent disregard for norms of general aesthetic interest, and possible status as an assault on the nation's cultural dignity) by targeting an arresting and already notorious picture that Léger had sent to the painting section of the Salon d'Automne. The newspaper reproduced this composition, entitled *Woman in Blue* (1912, Kunstmuseum, Basel), together with a three-item questionnaire on the "mystery" of cubist methods of representation: "Is this a painting? If this is a painting, does it represent something? If it represents something, what does it represent?" The outcome was more or less preprogrammed, since the editors attached a caption consisting of nothing but a line of question marks, graphic signs of incomprehension, and printed answers to the questionnaire mostly from old-guard painters associated with the Société des Artistes Français, the professional association that spoke for an "official" aesthetic sanctified by the administrative, intellectual, and educational establishment.[28]

Léger does not dwell in the Wassilieff lectures on the details of those recent art-world events, but they are there between the lines. And they were incontestably important to the more general and fundamental assessment of the situation of painting that he presented in his talks on painting in the era of its specialization. "Contrast" was the thread that connected his aesthetic preoccupations to his avant-gardist historical, moral, and, finally, social consciousness.

New Means of Production

To say that the First World War brought the *Contrasts* to an abrupt end is true and at the same time insufficient. The war changed everything for Léger. It unraveled the personal and institutional threads of his artistic life. Salons and gallery activities were suspended. The little magazines that defended cubism and avant-garde culture folded. The cubist groups broke up, their members hunkering down in Paris, leaving town, traveling abroad, or going into the service. Kahnweiler went to Switzerland, and the state moved to sequester the contents of his gallery; at one stroke Léger lost both the contract that made his livelihood and access to the largest part of his life work, now confiscated as part of Kahnweiler's stock. When the general war mobilization was declared on August 1, 1914, Léger was called up. He entered the Engineer Corps as a reservist (because he was in his early thirties and not a professional soldier), but this did not keep him from being sent quickly to the Western Front. He worked first as a military engineer digging fortifications in the already devastated Argonne forest and then, in October, was reassigned to an ambulance unit to work as a stretcher-bearer with the gruesome and dangerous task of clearing the field of the injured and the dead. Later, he served as a major's secretary and a cook.

Léger suffered the hardships of combat, and his letters from the front contain vivid descriptions of the rigors of the soldier's life: the constant miseries of rain and mud, feelings of monotony and fatigue, the shocks of bombardment. In a letter of November 1914 to his old friend Mare, now also a soldier, Léger put into words the predicament of an artist in the trenches. He began with a remark about the soldier's practice of stripping useful material from corpses and turned it into a grim joke about war as material for art.

> I spend five days a week no farther than eighty meters from the Germans and I don't think I'll ever get to see one alive. But here's something grim. I see plenty [of dead Germans] and take the swines' shoes, but no one has my size. My shoes hurt, theirs look comfortable. I haven't yet given up on the idea of bringing back a pair, naturally in order to make some still lifes for Kahnweiler's. The first month, I was sure I was going to die.[29]

This remark about Cubist still lifes from German shoes was perhaps intended as a wry retort to those critics who used to denigrate the new art as a conspiracy to corrupt the true culture of France and to attack Kahnweiler and other art dealers with Germano-Jewish names as the agents of this corruption. Coming as it did, in the early months of the war, the joke also underlined a simpler, more direct, and fairly dark question.

But the standstill created by his service in the war was only temporary. Léger resumed drawing after a ten-day furlough, which made possible a trip to his studio in September 1915. Once back in the Argonne forest, he took advantage of calm moments to record what he saw in pencil, ink, and watercolor drawings, many of which he clearly considered studies for more elaborate compositions. These drawings take up representative war themes: trench habitation, supply convoys, battlefields and ruined towns, and the soldiers. Léger also made a few paintings and a small number of pictures in oil and bits of brightly-colored pasted paper (a technique without precedent in his own work) laid over pieces of wood, some scavenged from used armament crates. Jeanne Lohy, Léger's future wife, who had stepped in to act as his intermediary for dealing with collectors in Paris, sold one of the wartime pictures to the Swedish painter Nils Dardel, who was scouting for artwork on behalf of a collector, the modern dancer Rolf de Maré. Léger wrote to Dardel to thank him and also to see if arrangements might be made for him to look at the few prewar canvases that remained in his studio, a group on the theme of staircase climbers. "These are fairly abstract investigations (contrasts of forms and colors)," Léger explained, choosing his words to highlight the experimental thrust of the paintings' manner, "which I was trying to develop fully in a large painting that would have been entitled *The Staircase*." This is followed in the letter by a reflection on the immediate and long-term impact of the war for his painting.

> The war took me and prevented me from accomplishing what I wanted. If I have the chance to continue my work, I'll get back to it with energy and with pleasure. The war came too late to influence me. I'll continue in the same vein and with the same tendencies. Excuse me for taking the liberty of writing, but I feel I have earned the right because you possess a work that I cared about a lot and which was made under bombardment. That's the sort of thing one doesn't forget.[30]

In spite of the disclaimer in his letter to Dardel—"The war came too late to influence me"—Léger was already quite convinced that the war had changed his way of understanding things. "I'm beginning to glimpse the enormity, from all points of view, of this gigantic war that we've undertaken," he wrote in November 1914 to the critic Maurice Raynal, another art-world comrade who was serving in the military. "This life in the squad, shoulder to shoulder with all these soldiers is already full of new things! We live in what is real, in objective utility. Bread, socks, meat: these simple things all have their intrinsic and true value."[31] Léger, quite conscious of his own status as a Parisian, an intellectual, and a worker in a luxury industry, took refuge in the myth of the *poilu*, the stalwart and masculine (literally, "hairy") French infantryman, as an ordinary hero and as the representative of an authentic frontline community. Léger admired the *poilu* for his vaunted resourcefulness in the face of material scarcity and his ability to persevere in the face of physical danger. He affected the *poilu*'s plebian slang and took up his characteristic behavior, beliefs, and ways of thinking. His attitude was a mixture of cheerful optimism and hard-headed pragmatism, fatalism in the face of death, an eschewal of home front war propaganda and official patriotic symbolism, and anger at the irresponsibility of life back home.[32]

But Léger's assertion of new feeling of objectivity, truthfulness, reality, and simplicity—all bound up in the circumstances of the war—also had prewar aesthetic roots. Léger came to see the war as a modern thing, and he defined its modernity according to the conceptual categories he used to think about art. Thus, if the war quickened perceptions of everything that was concrete and real, it also taught a lesson about abstraction, and the two were closely intertwined. In a letter written to a noncombatant friend, Léger explained how technology had turned killing into a set of calculations, complex, impersonal, unfeeling, and purely strategic. "It's as linear and dry as a geometry problem. A given number of bombs in a given time over a given area, a given number of men per meter, in perfect order and at a given time. Everything is triggered mechanically. It's pure abstraction, even purer than cubist painting itself. I won't hide my liking for that way of doing things . . . ."[33] Men and machines of war became prime subjects of Léger's wartime work, which culminated in *The Card Players* (Kröller-Müller Museum, Otterlo, 1917), painted during the convalescence that ended his active service. It is a study of three infantrymen, their bodies armored with gleaming geometrical forms, suggesting aggression barely restrained by their leisurely activity.

Léger's army service came to an end in June 1918, five months ahead of the armistice.[34] Half a year later, in a 1919 letter to Léonce Rosenberg, who had now replaced Kahnweiler as his art dealer in Paris, he turned his attention to the question of before and after, of prewar achievements and work to come.

> My artistic origins: influence of the impressionists, Renoir and Seurat, with respect to color; in terms of form, Ingres and David. Before the war, indecisiveness, struggle against influences and against standard taste, timidity, hesitation. Three years of war without touching a brush but in direct contact with reality at its most violent and coarse. After my discharge, I took advantage of those tough years and came to a decision.[35]

In other words: after a period of experimentation comes a period of consolidation. When we read statements like this one, about the war's transformative impact on Léger's art, we say to ourselves: how could he have thought of it any other way? We draw a line at the summer of 1914 to mark the conclusion of the first great phase in the painter's life's work and the beginning of the next one. However, a careful reading of the 1919 letter will temper any simple notion of change over time. This is evident in Léger's reference to artistic predecessors. His mention of Seurat reflects a general rise within postwar modernist circles of appreciation of this artist as a painter of order and control. The allusion to David, an artist whom Léger confessed to not understanding before the war, reflects his new estimation of an exemplary French classicist.[36] Still, it is worth noting that while Léger's sense of the polarities of style and meaning seem to have shifted with the new postwar moment, his habit of thinking about geometry and color in diametrical opposition is as strong as ever.

And so is the basic conceptual framework, based in the rhetoric of "contrast." This becomes clear as the 1919 letter to Rosenberg continues with a discussion of pictorial style:

> I model in pure color and large volumes, with no concessions. I mean to outshine tasteful arrangements, grey shadows, and dead backgrounds. I go for maximum pictorial output through the contrast of all available plastic resources. Never mind good manners, taste, and ordinary style. If my painting has any, we'll know later; right now I'm kicking up a fuss. For me painting must be all radiance and motion, and the very opposite of the wall. I am pleased when my painting dominates a room in an apartment, when it forces itself on everything, people and furniture. It must be the most important figure. I hate cautious painting.

Léger then returns once more to the question of subject matter.

> I take my subject matter from everywhere. I like the forms that modern industry imposes, and I make use of them: steel, with its thousands of colorful reflections, is subtler and steadier than so-called classical subjects. I maintain that a machine gun and the breech of a 75 cannon are greater subject matter for painting than four apples on a table or a Saint-Cloud landscape, and that's without practicing futurism.[37]

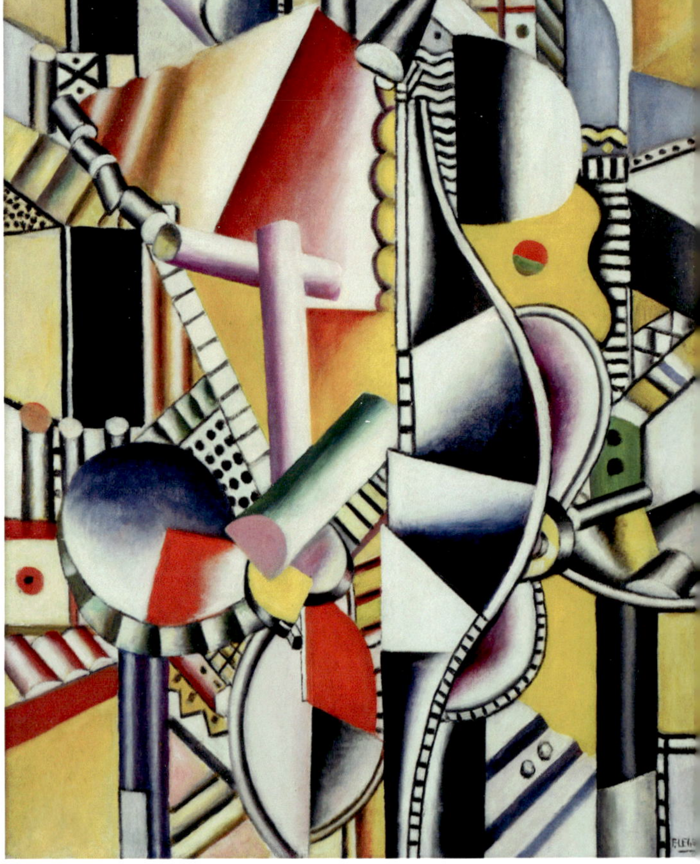

Figure 4. Fernand Léger (1881–1955). *Propellers,* 1918. Oil on canvas, 31⅞ x 25¾ in. (80.9 x 65.4 cm.). Katherine S. Dreier Bequest. (171.1953). The Museum of Modern Art, New York. *Digital Image © The Museum of Modern Art/Licensed by SCALA / Art Resource, NY*

This discussion of machine guns and cannons underscores an appreciation for specifically industrial objects, which emerged in the prewar period and was only intensified in wartime. The final remark, coming from an artist who had such important contacts with the Italian futurists, is most relevant as a way of underscoring his desire to balance dynamism and control in the construction of the motif.

Léger put these intentions into action in a substantial body of new work, comprising some fifty-seven paintings, watercolors, and drawings, which went on view at Rosenberg's Galerie "L'Effort Moderne" in February

1919.[38] The exhibition turned old ideas into new ones. Léger's favorite forming elements—the cylinders, cones, step motifs, conspicuous effects of luster—all returned. At the same time, the technique tightened up, the impetuous brush becoming smooth, the unfinished surface much more homogeneous and continuous. These aspects signaled a new emphasis on rational order. The exhibition referred back to the prewar work with a picture entitled *Contrasts of Forms* (1918, Musée d'Art Moderne de la Ville de Paris), an abstract arrangement with elements that suggest a townscape. It highlighted *The Card Game*, the major wartime painting. It charted the direction that Léger would take in the early 1920s, when he developed his aesthetic fascination for industrial objects and formulated his signature aesthetic of the machine. The exhibition explored a world of mechanized labor and production, the peace that came after an industrialized war. There were images of factories, tugboats, and motors. A picture entitled *Propellers* (1918, The Museum of Modern Art, fig. 4), presented an airplane propeller as the centerpiece of an array of rods, blades, discs, and corrugated planes. Here Léger's beautiful industrial object combines the dryness of geometry and the fantasy of color and reflected light. Curves oppose straight lines, flat elements line up against modeled ones, and a hard sheen counters the chromatic intensity of vermilions, blues, yellows, and greens.

The war's epochal character has weighed heavily on efforts to come to an historical understanding of the work Léger produced before and after it. But we will search in vain for a simple and straightforward change in Léger's approach to form and abstraction.[39] In effect, Léger was a patient, methodical worker. He thought in terms of sequences and series, steady elements of structure expressed in multiform ways. While he emphasized the industrial thing as an object of aesthetic perception during the war and in the years that immediately followed, that discovery was preceded and prepared for by his development of visual motifs based on contrasts of line, shape, color, and—most crucially—luster. All of that occurred in spectacular fashion in the course of creating the *Contrasts of Forms*.

Matthew Affron is Associate Professor in the McIntire Department of Art, University of Virginia, and Director of Special Curatorial Projects at the University of Virginia Art Museum.

[1] Douglas Cooper, *Léger: Contrastes de formes, 1912–1915* (Paris: Berggruen, 1962), n. pag. For the essential scholarship on the series since, see Christopher Green, *Léger and the Avant-Garde* (New Haven: Yale University Press, 1975); Virginia Spate, *Orphism: The Evolution of Non-Figurative Painting in Paris, 1910–1914* (Oxford: Clarenden Press, 1979), 250–274; Claude Laugier and Michèle Richet, *Léger: oeuvres de Fernand Léger, 1881–1955* (Paris: Centre Georges Pompidou, 1981), 23–24; Green, "Fernand Léger: *The Staircase (Second State)*," in *The European Avant-Gardes, Art in France and Western Europe, 1904–1945: The Thyssen-Bornemisza Collection* (London: Zwemmer, 1995), 274–279; and Christian Derouet, "Les 'Contrastes de formes,' 1912–1914," in *Fernand Léger* (Paris: Centre Georges Pompidou, 1997), 43–45.

[2] André Warnod, "Le Salon des Indépendants: fauves et cubistes," *Comoedia* (18 March 1913): 1. Unless otherwise noted, translations in this essay are by the author.

[3] On chiaroscuro drawing, see James Watrous, *The Craft of Old-Master Drawings* (Madison: University of Wisconsin Press, 1957), 34–43.

[4] A number of colored gouaches allegedly dated 1913 and 1914 appeared in the art market during the 1960s, and their authenticity was strongly disputed. See Eugene Victor Thaw, interviewed by Ronald D. Spencer, in *The Expert Versus the Object: Judging Fakes and False Attributions in the Visual Arts* (New York: Oxford University Press, 1994), 74.

[5] On luster and its representational functions, see E. H. Gombrich, "The Heritage of Apelles," in *The Heritage of Apelles: Studies in the Art of the Renaissance* (Ithaca: Cornell University Press, 1976), 3–18.

[6] See David Cottington, *Cubism and its Histories* (Manchester: Manchester University Press, 2004), esp. 167–172.

[7] On Kahnweiler's writing and its impact on cubist historiography, see: Werner Spies, "Vendre des tableaux—donner à lire," trans. Eliane Kaufholz, in *Daniel-Henry Kahnweiler* (Paris: Centre Georges Pompidou, 1984), 17–44; Daniel Robbins, "Abbreviated Historiography of Cubism," *Art Journal* 47, no. 4 (Winter 1988): 277–283; and Yve-Alain Bois, "Kahnweiler's Lesson," in *Painting as Model*, trans. Katharine Streip (Cambridge: The MIT Press, 1990), 65–97.

[8] This was the focus of a separate essay of the same year, Daniel Henry [Kahnweiler], "Fernand Léger," *Der Cicerone* 12 (October 1920): 699–702.

[9] Daniel-Henry Kahnweiler, *The Rise of Cubism*, trans. Henry Aronson (New York: Wittenborn, Schultz, Inc., 1949), 19; originally published as *Der Weg zum Kubismus* (Munich: Delphin-Verlag, 1920).

[10] Kahnweiler, *The Rise of Cubism*, 19.

[11] Léger, "Notes on the Mechanical Element" (1923), in *Functions of Painting*, trans. Alexandra Anderson, ed. Edward F. Fry (New York: The Viking Press, 1973), 29; originally published as "À propos de l'élément mécanique" in Fernand Léger, *Fonctions de la peinture*, ed. Roger Garaudy (Paris: Denoël-Gonthier, 1965), 50-52. This formulation of the "law of contrasts" would remain in force until the end of Léger's life; see the interview in André Verdet, *Entretiens: notes et écrits sur la peinture* (Paris: Editions du Petit Véhicule, 2000), 73.

[12] On Cézanne's color and the transformation of chiaroscuro, see Richard Shiff, *Cézanne and the End of Impressionism* (Chicago: University

of Chicago Press, 1984), 199–219; and David Summers, *Real Spaces: World Art History and the Rise of Western Modernism* (London: Phaidon, 2003), 627–630.

[13] Émile Bernard, "Paul Cézanne," *L'Occident* no. 32 (July 1904), reprinted in *Souvenirs sur Paul Cézanne* (Paris: Société des Trente, 1912); English translation in *Conversations with Cézanne*, ed. Michael Doran, trans. Julie Lawrence Cochran (Berkeley: University of California Press, 2000), 32–44. The published version of Léger's essay that contains the reference to Cézanne's aphorism is: Léger, "Les Origines de la peinture et sa valeur représentative," *Der Sturm* 4, no. 172–173 (August 1913): 78.

[14] Léger, "The Origins of Painting and its Representational Value" (1913), in *Functions of Painting*, 7; originally published as Léger, "Les Origines de la peinture et sa valeur représentative. Notes réunies pour une conférence," *Montjoie!*, 1, no. 8 (29 May 1913): 7; 1, no. 9/10 (14-29 June 1913): 9-10.

[15] On color in Picasso's work, See Linda Nochlin, "Picasso's Color: Schemes and Gambits," *Art in America* 68, no. 10 (December 1980): 105–121 and 177–183; and Rosalind E. Krauss, *The Picasso Papers* (Cambridge, MA: The MIT Press, 1999), esp. 162–192.

[16] Léger to Kahnweiler, 11 December 1919, in Kahnweiler, "Fernand Léger," *Burlington Magazine* 92, no. 564 (March 1950): 64.

[17] See Max Imdahl, "Delaunay's Position in History," in Gustav Vriesen and Max Imdahl, *Robert Delaunay: Light and Color* (New York: Harry N. Abrams, 1969), 71–86; and Georges Roque, *Art et science de la couleur: Chevreul et les peintres, de Delacroix à l'abstraction* (Nîmes: Éditions Jacqueline Chambon, 1997), 346–362.

[18] Robert Delaunay, "Le Petit cahier de Robert Delaunay" (1933), in *Du Cubisme à l'art abstrait*, ed. Pierre Francastel (Paris : S.E.V.P.E.N., 1957), 76.

[19] See *Robert Delaunay 1906–1914 : de l'impressionnisme à l'abstraction* (Paris: Centre Georges Pompidou, 1999), 19.

[20] Léger, "The Origins of Painting and its Representational Value," 10 (translation modified).

[21] Léger, "Contemporary Achievements in Painting" (1914), in *Functions of Painting*, 11; originally published as Léger, "Les Réalisations picturales actuelles," *Les Soirées de Paris* 3, no. 25 (15 June 1914): 349-356.

[22] See Pär Bergman, *"Modernolatria" et "Simultaneità": recherches sur deux tendances dans l'avant-garde littéraire en Italie et en France à la veille de la première guerre mondiale* ([Stockholm]: Svenska Bokforläget, 1962), esp. 261–411; and Cottington, *Cubism and its Histories*, 85-104.

[23] Léger, "Contemporary Achievements in Painting," 12.

[24] See Robert L. Herbert, "Léger's *Le Grand Déjeuner*," in *From Millet to Léger: Essays in Social Art History* (New Haven: Yale University Press, 2002), 129; and Georges Roque, "Harmonie des couleurs, harmonie sociale," *48/14: La revue du Musée d'Orsay* no. 12 (Spring 2001): 62–73.

[25] Léger, "Contemporary Achievements in Painting," 12, 13, and 14.

[26] Charles Beauquier, "L'Affiche, voilà l'ennemi!" *La Publicité* 9, no. 94 (May 1911): 149-150; and *Journal officiel* (3 December 1912): 2925.

[27] See Nancy J. Troy, *Modernism and the Decorative Arts in France: Art Nouveau to Le Corbusier* (New Haven: Yale University Press, 1991), 79–98; and David Cottington, "The Maison Cubiste and the Meaning of Modernism in Pre-1914 France," in *Architecture and Cubism*, eds. Eve Blau and Nancy Troy (Cambridge, MA: The MIT Press, 1997), 17–40.

[28] "Le Mystère cubiste," *L'Eclair* (19 October 1912): 1. On this debate, the poster controversy and the larger issue of public perceptions of cubist painting, see Jeffrey S. Weiss, *The Popular Culture of Modern Art: Picasso, Duchamp, and Avant-Gardism* (New Haven: Yale University Press, 1994), 49–105.

[29] Léger to André Mare, 17 November 1914, Documentation (LEG C7 8827), Musée National d'Art Moderne, Paris.

[30] Léger to Nils Dardel, 14 November 1915, in *Fernand Léger: une correspondance de guerre à Louis Poughon, 1914–1918* (Paris: Editions du Centre Georges Pompidou, 1990), 97, n. 22.

[31] Léger to Maurice Raynal, 14 November 1914, in *Fernand Léger* (1997), 303.

[32] See Christopher Green, "Out of War: Léger's Painting of the War and the Peace, 1914–1920," in *Fernand Léger, 1911–1924: The Rhythm of Modern Life*, ed. Dorothy Kosinski (Munich: Prestel, 1994), 44–55; Éric Michaud, "Art, War, Competition: The Three Battles of Fernand Léger," in *Fernand Léger, 1911–1924: The Rhythm of Modern Life*, 56–63; and Stéphane Audoin-Rouzeau, "La Correspondance de guerre de Fernand Léger en 1914–1918," *Europe* no. 818–819 (June-July 1997), 51–57.

[33] Léger to Louis Poughon, 30 May 1915, in *Fernand Léger: une correspondance de guerre à Louis Poughon, 1914–1918*, 36.

[34] It had long been thought (following his own statements) that Léger was gassed at Verdun, but the record is corrected in the two volumes of letters that are now the best documentary sources on Léger's life in the army and in the decade afterward. In July 1915 Léger had a shrapnel leg wound and in 1917 he was hospitalized for treatment of nervous gastritis, rheumatism, and pulmonary tuberculosis. See *Fernand Léger: une correspondance de guerre à Louis Poughon*, 4; and *Fernand Léger: une correspondance d'affaires, 1917–1937*, ed. Christian Derouet (Paris: Centre Georges Pompidou, 1996), 27.

[35] Léger to Léonce Rosenberg, prior to 27 January 1919, in *Fernand Léger: une correspondance d'affaires*, 47. Rosenberg published an extract from this letter in the Italian journal *Valori Plastici* 1, nos. 2–3 (January-February 1919): 3; he published it more fully and with the addition of passages from a letter of September 1921 (and gave this new, pieced-together text the date 1922) in *Bulletin de l'Effort Moderne* no. 4 (April 1924): 10–11.

[36] On Seurat's postwar reputation, see Kenneth E. Silver, *Esprit de Corps: The Art of the Parisian Avant-Garde and the First World War, 1914-1925* (Princeton: Princeton University Press, 1989), 336–339. Léger remembers his uncomprehending reaction to the David exhibition at the Palais des Beaux-Arts de la Ville de Paris in 1913 in Raymond Cogniat, "Chez Fernand Léger," *Beaux-Arts* (21 April 1933): 2.

[37] Léger to Rosenberg, prior to 27 January 1919, in *Fernand Léger: une correspondance d'affaires*, 47.

[38] The exhibition catalogue is reprinted in *Fernand Léger: une correspondance d'affaires*, 284–294.

[39] See Gladys C. Fabre, "The Modern Spirit and the Problem of Abstraction for Léger, his Friends and his Students at the *Académie Moderne*," trans. Michael Walsh, in *Léger and the Modern Spirit* (Paris: Musée d'Art Moderne de la Ville de Paris/Houston: Museum of Fine Arts, 1982), 407–429; Green, "Out of War: Léger's Painting of the War and the Peace, 1914–1920"; and Maria Gough's "*Ciné-graphie*: On Fernand Léger's drawings, 1912–14," in the present volume, 19-25.

Ciné-graphie: On Fernand Léger's Drawings, 1912–14

MARIA GOUGH

Réalisme pictural

In the history of modern drawing, the period just before the First World War stands out for numerous reasons, not least for the radicalization of the pictorial support affected by Georges Braque and Pablo Picasso between 1912 and 1914 in their collaboratively invented art of *papiers collés*. Pasted fragments of faux-bois wallpaper and other mass-produced papers, pages torn from the daily newspaper, and even (though much more rarely) whole photographs became not only the ground for their charcoal and ink, but also their "graphic" medium per se. Juan Gris, another cubist also promoted by their enterprising young dealer, Daniel-Henry Kahnweiler, soon followed suit, producing a significant body of new work. Lone among Kahnweiler's cubists never to adopt the technique, however, was Fernand Léger, perhaps because, as he later confided, "[c]omposition achieved by assembled surfaces, which is the characteristic of cubist pictures, has never been my forte."[1]

As the eleven drawings in the present exhibition demonstrate, Léger's support during the heyday of *papiers collés* was unremarkable: ordinary sheets of once off-white paper cut to more or less standard dimensions, their surfaces slick to the brush. At this crucial moment in the history of drawing, Léger's graphic energy was directed not toward a radicalization of the ground, it seems fair to suggest, but rather toward a liberation of its traditional wet media. One of the most immediately striking aspects of these drawings is their sheer painterliness.[2] Loaded with black ink or watercolor, Léger's brush arcs up and down and back and forth across each sheet, constructing a multiplicative, contrapuntal rhythm that intersects, at almost every turn, an irregular scaffolding of straight lines. The same brush also produces fluid planes of solid black pigment and vigorous passages of hatching; to both are counterposed areas of thick impasto in brilliant white gouache or oil. The result: painterly constructions in black and white.

These dynamic works on paper belong to an extensive, highly experimental series known collectively as the *Contrasts of Forms* (*Contrastes de formes*), which Léger produced in Paris between late 1912 and mid-1914. Comprising around fifty canvases and one hundred drawings, the *Contrasts* constitute Léger's first substantial body of work, or, perhaps it would be more accurate to say, the earliest substantial corpus to which we now have access.[3] Yet the series has been surprisingly little analyzed in the literature, as Christian Derouet notes.[4] No doubt this neglect has to do with the way in which the *Contrasts* broach the matter of abstraction, which is generally considered an exceptional rather than a typical preoccupation within Léger's oeuvre overall. Notwithstanding this exceptionality, the *Contrasts* establish Léger as a fundamental figure for any consideration of the complex place of abstraction within the various cubisms thriving in Paris before the First World War.

Most of the exhibited drawings were preparatory for paintings on canvas. For each major oil in the series, Léger would produce a sequence of preliminary drawings and through this process would arrive at a definitive version of a given composition. But some drawings in the series seem to have been more free-wheeling, as though unleashed by the process of drawing itself. One of the great virtues of the exhibited selection is that it is representative of the multiple avenues Léger explored in the *Contrasts*, simultaneously rather than sequentially, it would seem. Consider, for example, the comparatively normative spatial depth and iconographical legibility of *Two Reclining Women* (1913, cat. 5) or *Study for "Still Life"* (1913, cat. 8), with the way in which Léger pushes that same pictorial vocabulary of arcs and straight lines to the brink of total illegibility in *Study for "Contrast of Forms"* (1913, cat. 6), *Contrast of Forms* (1913, cat. 7), and *Composition (Contrast of Forms)* (1912–13, cat. 4). Considered alongside a whole phalanx of comparable drawings of which it is representative, *Composition (Contrast of Forms)*—a drawing of extraordinary graphic force (and, for this writer, the strongest work in the exhibition)—presents a compelling argument for Léger as a pioneer of abstraction.[5]

It is important to note, however, that Léger himself seems not to have divvied up the *Contrasts* according to the presence or absence of recognizable motifs, but instead tended to think of the entire series under the rubric of abstraction. In a November 1915 letter to the Swedish artist Nils Dardel, for example, he describes three paintings on the theme of *The Staircase* as attempts "at something rather abstract (contrasts of forms and colors)."[6] This description is intriguing because Léger's works on this subject—two of which are included in the present exhibition (1913; cats. 9 and 10)—are manifestly referential. Elsewhere, Léger asserts that he departed for the front in 1914 "in the middle of an abstract style, a time of pictorial liberation,"[7] but that the war had made him "forget [all about] the abstract art of 1912–13."[8] Such comments prompt one to ask: What does the notion of abstraction signify for Léger in 1912–14?

To begin to answer this question we might consider the artist's first public statements about modern painting and his relation to it, which took the form of two lectures presented at the Academy Wasilieff in Paris in May 1913 and May 1914, contemporaneously with his production of the *Contrasts*.[9] In neither text does Léger deploy the word "abstract."[10] But he does attack with considerable vigor the priority given to the referent in the history of "visual realism" [*réalisme visuel*] or "imitation," and to advocate that that priority now be transferred to the formal elements of painting itself. The 1913 lecture begins with Léger ridiculing the perennial question asked of the work of art—"What does [it] represent?"—as but an "utter inanity." In the place of visual realism, Léger proposes an art of "pictorial realism" [*réalisme pictural*], which he defines as the "simultaneous ordering [*ordonnation*] of three great plastic components: Lines, Forms, and Colors" (3–4).*

It is the particular nature of this "ordering" that is most at issue for Léger, for it is a dynamic of "contrasts" that governs the compositional praxis not only of his own work but also that of the recent past: "Pictorial contrasts used in their purest sense (complementary colors, lines and forms)," he argues, "are . . . the structural basis of modern pictures" (7). There is a passage in John Ruskin's *The Elements of Drawing* (1857) where the author notes that the "law of contrast" is simply a way of exemplifying the characteristics of things;[11] for Léger, however, "modern" contrasts exemplify not things but the plastic components of painting itself. Léger also distinguishes his own production of contrast from even that of its more recent practitioners, such as Paul Signac, by his acute emphasis on its dissonant, even violent quality: "Contrast = dissonance" (16), he declares.

Despite his emphasis on painting's plastic elements, at no point in the 1913 lecture does Léger propose the suppression of the referent altogether, though the thrust of his polemic certainly moves in that direction. (Kazimir Malevich would soon transform Léger's concept of *réalisme pictural* into full-blown nonobjectivity, in his declaration of Suprematism as "painterly realism" [*zhivopisnyi realizm*] as opposed to painterly illusionism, at the 0.10 Exhibition he co-organized in St. Petersburg in 1915.)[12] But in the 1914 lecture Léger clarifies the issue, insisting not on the referent's elimination but its instrumentalization. Ever since the impressionists' "liberation of painting" from visual realism, he writes, "the modern picture set out at once to structure itself on contrasts; instead of submitting to a subject, the painter . . . uses a subject in the service of purely plastic means" (14). This assertion also supports his contestation of the Futurist emphasis on modern subject matter ("locomotives and other modern engines"). Modernity, Léger argues, can be delivered via the "most banal, worn-out subject, like a nude in a studio and a thousand others . . . The only interesting thing is how [that subject] is used" (17). For Léger himself, then, abstraction is not so much an ontological category defined in terms of the presence or absence of referentiality, as it would soon become for Malevich and Mondrian, but rather a mode of production in which explicit emphasis is placed on the formal properties of the medium. When Léger writes to his childhood friend Louis Poughon in May 1915, confiding that the technology of modern warfare had confronted him with "pure abstraction, purer than cubist painting,"[13] it seems that here the artist himself acknowledges the impurity, if we may call it that, of his own abstraction.

* As stated in endnote 9, numbers in parentheses refer to pages in the cited source.

Chez Kahnweiler

The *Contrasts* were produced during the period in which Léger formally consolidated his relationship with Kahnweiler, who maintained exclusive agreements with a number of other artists before the war, most notably Georges Braque, Juan Gris, Pablo Picasso, André Derain, and Maurice Vlaminck. According to these contracts, each artist agreed to sell his work only to Kahnweiler and at prices pre-established according to the size of the canvas or sheet; in return, the latter agreed to purchase everything the artist produced. With such economic security, the pressure to produce a successful "manifesto" for display at the typically crowded salon—a pressure that Léger had apparently keenly felt in the months preceding the Salon des Indépendants of 1911—was off. Furthermore, after mounting just three shows at his modest rue Vignon gallery—the third and final one in fall 1908 (comprising Braque's groundbreaking L'Estaque landscapes)—Kahnweiler no longer even held exhibitions, opting instead for unannounced "hangings" of selected paintings and conserving his energies for the expedition of works to exhibitions abroad. Kahnweiler's innovative model of patronage and exhibition practice enabled a different rhythm or temporality for artistic production than that established by the twice-yearly salons and gallery exhibitions alike, one much less punctuated or interrupted—depending on how one looks at it—by dates, details, obligations, logistics, and publicity.

It can plausibly be argued, therefore, that Kahnweiler facilitated Léger's sustained attention to the production of the *Contrasts* over the course of two years, guaranteeing their experimental quality and diversity. One difficulty with this scenario, however, is that it is a little unclear as to precisely when Léger became a rue Vignon artist. Kahnweiler signed an exclusive contract with Léger for three years in August 1913, but this fact alone does not give us a definitive date for the inception of their business relationship, since we know that Kahnweiler formalized his relationships with his other artists only years after their inception.[14] That said, the provenance of individual pictures can assist in establishing a provisional date of late 1912 or early 1913, contemporary with the first *Contrasts,* since this is when Kahnweiler's acquisition of Léger's work seems to have begun in earnest.[15] (Prior to that date, he had bought several paintings from Léger, including such major works as *Woman Sewing* [1909–10, Musée National d'Art Moderne, Paris], *Nudes in the Forest* [Kröller-Müller Museum, Otterlo, 1911], and *Woman in Blue* [1912, Kunstmuseum, Basel], but only after their exhibition at the salon, rather than directly from the artist's studio.)

The relationship between Léger and Kahnweiler is provocative for at least two reasons. First, it represents the presence of a leading salon cubist within the gallery cubist group, thereby to some extent confounding the binary division that has driven both sides of the debate over so-called true cubism, ever since Douglas Cooper and John Golding first introduced that term. Second, and more important for the present essay, is the fact that the drawings for the *Contrasts* are among the most abstract—in the inflected sense already discussed—that Léger ever produced. Yet Kahnweiler is renowned for his blanket condemnation of abstraction, whether as a characterization of cubism, or as a major tendency within twentieth-century art more generally. In this condemnation, Kahnweiler shares with many of his contemporaries (most notoriously, for example, Carl Einstein) a profound fear that abstraction collapses easel painting into decoration or ornament. The resolution of this grand irony—Kahnweiler as the patron of what he most feared—is that, unlike Léger, he mostly refused to see the *Contrasts* as abstract. To shed light on this matter, it is worth revisiting Kahnweiler's early commentary on the artist.

In addition to his practice as a dealer, Kahnweiler had an influential role as a critic and continues to be widely regarded as the most astute of the early writers on cubism. His career as a critic began in 1915 in Switzerland, while he was studying the philosophy of art at the University of Bern. During this period of tremendous uncertainty as to the fate of his rue Vignon gallery and its contents—as an enemy national he was unable to return to Paris until the war was over—Kahwneiler drafted a book-length manuscript deeply informed by his study of Kant and contemporary neo-Kantians, *Der Gegenstand der Aesthetik* (1915), which included three chapters on cubism. In these chapters, Kahnweiler offers an account of the development of cubism as a reaction against impressionism and post-impressionism in the name of a dialectic of depth and surface, or, in his own terminology, the reconciliation of the conflict between representation and structure. The first considers the early work of Picasso and Braque, the second the years of their closest collaboration, and the third cubism's "offshoots," by which he means the work of Marcel Duchamp and the Italian futurists. Revised versions of the first two of these chapters appeared in the Berlin periodical *Die weissen Blätter* in September 1916 under the pseudonym Daniel Henry.

It is only after the end of the war, however, that Kahnweiler puts into print for the first time his thoughts about the other major artists of his Paris gallery. Beginning in fall 1919, he publishes a sequence of breezy essays, first on Derain (October 1919), then on Vlaminck (December 1919), again on Derain (April 1920), and finally, on Léger (in *Der Cicerone* in October 1920). The character of these short pieces is distinct from that of his earlier manuscript, reading more like advance publicity as he prepares to relocate back to Paris in the hopes of establishing a new gallery (in collaboration with his friend and backer André Simon) and buying back at least some of his confiscated stock from the French state.

But in 1920 Kahnweiler also publishes his first book, *Der Weg zum Kubismus*, which was translated into English in 1949 as *The Rise of Cubism*.[16] The bulk of the book is an expansion of the 1916 *Die weissen Blätter* texts to which he also adds a short chapter on Léger and a revised version of the 1915 manuscript chapter on cubism's offshoots.[17] Thus dropped into a pre-existing narrative of cubism, Léger is presented (rather oxymoronically) as a belated pioneer [*Wegbereiter*] who, although not present at the movement's inception, nevertheless produced his own form of cubism under the stimulus of that of Picasso and Braque (17). Presented as pioneer rather than offshoot, Léger is sequestered from both the salon cubists and the Italian futurists. It is important to note the rhetorical function of the Léger chapter within *The Rise of Cubism* overall insofar as it reveals as much about Kahnweiler's convictions about cubism's relation to abstraction as it does about Léger's work itself.

According to Kahnweiler, Léger is a cubist in two major senses. First, his work has its origins in visual experience [*Seherlebnis*]: Despite the fact that his rendering of the object is "much more arbitrary" than that of Picasso and Braque, Kahnweiler writes, Léger never "succumb[s] to the delusion of 'abstract art,' which is only ornamental," because in his work there is "always a point of departure grounded in visual experience." Sometimes Léger "strays far from this point," however, "indulging" in "variations on a theme," producing thereby an "architecture of form" that no longer conveys the original visual experience. His goal becomes, instead, the painting itself, to which all else is subordinated. But even if Léger does sometimes attach "too exclusive a significance to the 'unity' [*'Einheit'*] of the painting at the expense of the diversity of visual experience," Kahnweiler concludes, his work is "still cubism" because "adherence to visual experience" remains its fundamental "basis" (18).

This first point is essential to Kahnweiler's second and more contentious argument that Léger's adherence to visual experience is adherence "in the Cubist sense" (18) because he endeavors to reproduce the three-dimensional "diversity" of the external world on a two-dimensional field. Kahnweiler thus places Léger squarely within the dialectical struggle that he believes drives the development of cubism overall. "Representation and structure conflict" (1). Cubism reconciles this conflict. Its dialectical attention to both the representation of depth and the articulation of surface distinguishes cubism from what Kahnweiler considers to be the absolute or undialectical flatness—"playing cards" is his pejorative term—of Édouard Manet, Paul Gauguin, and Henri Matisse. So keen is Kahnweiler to insist on the "dimension of depth" that he even concedes a point to the hostile critic Louis Vauxcelles, who had coined the term cubism in a negative review of Braque's rue Vignon exhibition of fall 1908: "As the silly name 'Cubism' put it, with accidental correctness," Kahnweiler writes, "Braque and Picasso emphasize the cubic" (18).

Kahnweiler proposes that Léger is committed to the same project of the reconciliation of surface and depth, but by "other means": "simplif[ying] and coarsen[ing] forms," Léger "returns them to shapes most closely resembling the basic forms of cube, sphere, and cylinder," and is "always careful to preserve the closed form, never reaching the point of rupturing it." As a result, a Léger figure is a "huge Golem, an ungainly puppet . . . [Léger] offers the spectator big lumpish syntheses imprisoned in a cyclopian, piled-up structure" (18).[18] Léger's "forms are molded [*gemodelt*] and arched [*gewölbt*] through chiaroscuro in the simplest [*einfachste*], most significant [*prägnanteste*] way. Light serves only to depict form. This is done with the greatest possible emphasis by lighting one side and shading the other"(18). Placing chiaroscuro at the center of Léger's project of reconciliation, Kahnweiler thus defines its function in the traditional terms of the tonal modeling of volume.

Kahnweiler concludes that, "to some extent," therefore, Léger shares the same tendencies as Picasso and Braque in the pioneering phase of their cubism of 1908–09 (for example, the aforementioned L'Estaque landscapes, or Picasso's *Three Women* [State Hermitage Museum, St. Petersburg, 1908]). The text is non-specific but Léger's *Nudes in the Forest* (1909–10) would seem to be most exemplary of this shared commonality. Each of these works boasts a kind of bas-relief sculptural illusion, indicative of an effort to represent the diversity of the three-dimensional world, to use Kahnweiler's phraseology. One of their key tools is chiaroscuro, deployed in its traditional function of modeling, but it is equally used to undermine that illusion. The intensification of value contrasts and the presence of multiple and conflicting light sources tend to undermine the opposition of figure and ground essential for perception (hence our difficulty in distinguishing, in *Nudes in the Forest*, for example, between animate and inanimate forms, between bodies and vegetation). In undermining that cardinal opposition, Léger thereby draws attention to the surface on which that illusion is produced. In other words, we have a (cubist) reconciliation of the conflict between representation and structure.

It is unclear how well this early model of cubism describes Léger's *Contrasts,* which is Kahnweiler's larger intent in the chapter. While his reference to the iconography of the Golem may encompass not only the three figures lunging in *Nudes in the Forest*, but also the tubularized figures descending or ascending staircases in 1913–14 (for example, *Study for "The Staircase"* [1913, cat. 10]), it suppresses the dramatic formal differences between Léger's early salon cubism and his later gallery cubism.

The book had a composite nature and the Léger chapter was a later addition. This no doubt goes some of the way to explaining Kahnweiler's largely static account of Léger, especially when compared with the developmental narrative afforded Picasso and Braque. The latter two, according to Kahnweiler's own perspicacious commentary, transcended their own early cubism in the wake of Picasso's crisis at Cadaqués in summer 1910, piercing the closed form as Kahnweiler famously puts it (10), and henceforth disassociating chiaroscuro from its traditional descriptive function as tonal modeling. The sole place where Kahnweiler does acknowledge development in Léger is with respect to color: his shift from harmonious and delicate hues in 1911 to the strident and arbitrary colors of 1912 onwards. But the more crucial reason for Kahnweiler's one-sided presentation of the later work is what we might think of as a certain resistance to the *Contrasts*, on the critic's part, due to his aforementioned hostility to abstraction, a hostility that he compulsively reiterates throughout *The Rise of Cubism*. It is this hostility that drives Kahnweiler to interpret their chiaroscuro as sculptural illusion, effectively blinding him to the way in which the *Contrasts* transcend Léger's own earlier pictorial practice.

Ciné-graphie

This is not to suggest that the *Contrasts* afford no sense of volume, only that it is line—the vigorous arc of the loaded brush—that creates that volume rather than chiaroscuro. This is especially the case in the early "planar" compositions, such as *Study for "Nude Model in the Studio"/Composition I* (1912, cat. 2), but it is also true of *Composition (Contrast of Forms)* (1912–13, cat. 4) and the more Golem-like—to use Kahnweiler's metaphor—productions of 1914. The function of chiaroscuro is not so much to model volume, I would argue, as to interrogate the convention of tonal modeling itself. By hypostatizing chiaroscuro's most elementary property, that of value, into its two most extreme or contrasted states—brilliant black, brilliant white (rather than, as Kahnweiler might have it, shadow and light)—and eliminating any transitional negotiations between the two states, Léger lays bare this most fundamental technique of visual illusion—chiaroscuro raw, as it were, not so much the modeler of the figure of the Golem but the raw material (the mud) from which that figure is fashioned by human hand. In fact,

Léger's *Contrasts* confound the opposition of matter and form that underwrites the story of the Golem by presenting matter now as form, for it is matter itself—the sheer contrast of pigments—that interrupts the surface of the sheet, animating it with an insistent, rhythmic flicker. By laying bare that system of value, the *Contrasts* enliven the support, ridding modernist painting of the "dead surface" that plagues, Léger asserts, visual realism.

In their graphic animation of the surface, the *Contrasts* could be seen to engage less in a dialectic of depth and surface—*pace* Kahnweiler—than in the project of medium specificity that Léger himself lays out in his 1913 lecture. Such a shoring up of the specificity of the medium is necessitated, Léger argues, by the proliferation of new media, such as photography and, most recently, the cinema: "The means of expression have," quite simply, "multiplied" (10). The problem, as Léger sees it, is that with respect to visual realism the capacity of these newer media far exceeds anything achieved to date by painting: How can narrative and historical salon painting, he asks, "compete with the screen of any cinema. Visual realism has never been so intensely captured. . . . [T]he few workers who used to be seen in the museums, planted in front of a cavalry charge . . . or a historical scene . . . are no longer there; they are at the cinema" (9). The only salvation for the older visual arts, therefore, is self-criticism: "[b]y limiting each discipline to its own purpose, it enables achievements to be intensified" (10).

Harking back to Gotthold Ephraim Lessing in 1766, and projecting forward to Clement Greenberg in 1940,[19] Léger's argument belongs to a long history of efforts to formulate what is specific to each medium out of competition with what it is not. But the *Contrasts* themselves confound that effort as much as they embody it, I want to suggest, in their animation of the sheet, in its compulsive, pulsatile flickering on and off. By means of a painterly graphic medium—itself already a hybrid—Léger creates, in short, a cinematic effect. Thus, the drawings themselves, in precisely their attention to their own "plastic components," suggest a discourse with, rather than quarantine from, the newer medium of cinema. While my argument might seem to contradict Léger's own highly articulate theorization of his practice within a project of medium specificity, it is bolstered, laterally as it were, by a parallel argument running through those very same lectures, wherein the *Contrasts* find their raison d'être not just in the medium but in the conditions of everyday life: for Léger, the contrastive dissonance of the series speaks directly to the contrastive dissonance of modern social life and metropolitan space.

In 1931, the German playwright Bertolt Brecht proposed an alternative model of the relationship between the traditional media and the newer so-called technological media, a model no longer rooted in the claims of specificity: "The old forms of transmission [*übermittlung*] are not unaffected by the newly emerging ones nor do they survive [in their old form] alongside them. The film viewer reads stories differently. But the storywriter views films too."[20] Brecht's implication, therefore, is that the storyteller now writes differently as well. But his point is not to suggest that the novelist should now imitate the cinema—a common enough phenomenon at the time and one he abhors as a degradation of both media—but rather that the advent of cinema spurs the revitalization of the novel. According to his friend and interlocutor Walter Benjamin, it was in the interest of a discourse with radio and cinema that Brecht himself stripped his own major medium of theater back to its podium.[21] Building on Brecht's argument, I would argue that the emergence of cinema, with its drama of moving light and shadow, prompted Léger to a laying bare of the pictorial convention of chiaroscuro in the *Contrasts*. But if so, it must equally be noted that cinema itself, in the wake of the *Contrasts*, is not left intact, at least not in Léger's hands. One has only to recall the multiplicative rhythm of his own first film, *Ballet Mécanique* (1924), a pioneering attack on visual realism in the very medium with which that realism was increasingly, and triumphantly, associated. Thus, if the *papiers collés* of his fellow cubists chez Kahnweiler radicalized the support and thus the medium of drawing, the achievement of Léger's *Contrasts* was to have demonstrated the early, historical concatenation of abstraction and cinema, before that link was sundered in the late 1920s with the consolidation of narrative cinema.

Maria Gough is Associate Professor in the Department of Art and Art History, Stanford University.

My thanks to Matthew Affron for kindly inviting me to contribute to this volume, and for numerous stimulating and informative conversations.

1 Fernand Léger to Daniel-Henry Kahnweiler, December 11, 1919, quoted in Daniel-Henry Kahnweiler, "Fernand Léger," *Burlington Magazine* 92, no. 564 (March 1950): 64.

2 The one exception in this selection is the charcoal drawing *Contrast of Forms* (1912, cat. 3).

3 At some point in the early 1910s, Léger destroyed most of his work dating to before 1908.

4 Christian Derouet, "Les 'Contrastes de formes,' 1912–1914," in *Fernand Léger* (Paris: Centre Georges Pompidou, 1997), 45. An exception to this neglect, however, is Christopher Green, *Léger and the Avant-garde* (New Haven: Yale University Press, 1976).

5 For example, *Contrast of Forms* (1913), ink and gouache on paper, private collection; reproduced in *Fernand Léger*, 51, fig. 6.

6 Quoted in Christopher Green, "Out of War: Léger's Painting of the War and the Peace, 1914–1920," in *Fernand Léger, 1911–1924: The Rhythm of Modern Life*, ed. Dorothy Kosinski (Munich and New York: Prestel, 1994), 47.

7 Quoted in Green, "Out of War: Léger's Painting of the War and the Peace, 1914–1920," 45.

8 Quoted in Dieter Koeppelin, "*Les Éléments mécaniques*: The Bridge between Léger's Pre- and Post-War Work," in *Fernand Léger, 1911–1924*, 221, note 10.

9 See Fernand Léger, "Les Origines de la peinture et sa valeur représentative: Notes réunies pour une Conférence faite à l'Académie Wassilieff, le samedi 5 mai 1913," *Montjoie! organe de l'impérialisme artistique français* 1, no. 8 (May 29, 1913) and nos. 9–10 (June 19, 1913): 9–10; trans. Alexandra Anderson in Fernand Léger, *Functions of Painting*, ed. Edward Fry (New York: Viking Press, 1973), 3–10; and Fernand Léger, "Les réalisations picturales actuelles: Conférence faite à l'Académie Wassilieff" [May 9, 1914], *Les Soirées de Paris* 3, no. 25 (June 1914): 349–357, trans. Alexandra Anderson in Léger, *Functions of Painting*, 11–19. Hereafter, page citations (to the English translations only) will be made in parentheses in the body of the text.

10 For the sake of precision I should note that Léger does use the word "abstraction" once in his 1914 lecture, when he writes that his theory of pictorial contrasts is "not an abstraction," but rather a formulation based on empirical observation; see Léger, *Functions of Painting*, 16. This is obviously a different usage of the word than the one with which we are concerned here.

11 "Of course the character of everything is best manifested by Contrast. Rest can only be enjoyed after labour; sound to be heard clearly, must rise out of silence; light is exhibited by darkness, darkness by light; and so on in all things. Now in art every colour has an opponent colour, which, if bought near it, will relieve it more completely than any other; so, also, every form and line may be made more striking to the eye by an opponent form or line near them; a curved line is set of by a straight one, a massy form by a slight one, and so on; and in all good work nearly double the value, which any given colour or form would have uncombined, is given to each by contrast"; see John Ruskin, *The Elements of Drawing* (New York: Watson-Gunthill Publications, 1997), 144.

12 Kazimir Malevich, *Ot kubizma i futurizma k suprematizmu: novyi zhivopisnyi realizm*, 3d ed. (Moscow, 1916), reprinted in *Kazimir Malevich: Stat'i, manifesty, teoreticheskie sochineniia i drugie raboty. 1913–1929,* 5 vols., ed. Aleksandra Shatskikh (Moscow: Gileia, 1995), vol. 1, 53; trans. John Bowlt as "From Cubism and Futurism to Suprematism: The New Painterly Realism," in *Russian Art of the Avant-garde: Theory and Criticism*, ed. John Bowlt, rev. ed. (New York: Thames & Hudson, 1988), 133. Malevich asserts that his "new painterly realism is a painterly one precisely because it has no realism of mountains, sky, water." Up until now, "there has been a realism of objects, but not of painterly, colored units."

13 Quoted in Green, "Out of War: Léger's Painting of the War and the Peace, 1914–1920," 50.

14 See *Daniel-Henry Kahnweiler* (Paris: Centre Georges Pompidou, 1984), 113, 119.

15 See the provenance for plates 23–66 in Georges Bauquier, *Fernand Léger: catalogue raisonné* (Paris: Maeght, 1990), vol. 1. It was not until November 1913, however, that Kahnweiler first shipped a Léger painting to an exhibition abroad; see "Von Daniel-Henry Kahnweiler beschickte Ausstellungen 1910–1914," in *Hommage à Kahnweiler* (Kaiserslautern: Pfalzgalerie, 1970), 69, 70.

16 Daniel-Henry Kahnweiler, *Der Weg zum Kubismus* (Munich: Delphin-Verlag, 1920), trans. Henry Aronson as *The Rise of Cubism* (New York: Wittenborn, Schultz, 1949).

17 A further chapter on Gris was added in the revised second edition of *Der Weg zum Kubismus*, published in Leipzig in 1929.

18 Within Jewish folklore, the Golem was a giant figure fashioned out of mud and animated by Rabbi Judah Loew ben Bezalel in sixteenth-century Prague; in the early twentieth century, the Golem was disseminated into mass culture via the Austrian writer Gustav Meyrink's novel *Der Golem* (1915) and the German actor-director Paul Wegener's pioneering horror movie of the same (1920). Both folkloric and mass-cultural references in the *Contrasts* prompted Kahnweiler's comment.

19 See Gotthold Ephraim Lessing, *Laocoön: An Essay on the Limits of Painting and Poetry* (1766); and Clement Greenberg, "Towards a Newer Laocoön" (1940), in Francis Frascina (ed.), *Pollock and After: The Critical Debate* (London: Harper & Row, 1985), 35–46.

20 Bertolt Brecht, "The Threepenny Lawsuit: A Sociological Experiment" (1931), in *Bertolt Brecht on Film and Radio*, ed. and trans. Marc Silberman (London: Methuen, 2000), 161.

21 See Walter Benjamin, "The Author as Producer" (1934), trans. Edmund Jephcott, in *Selected Writings*, vol. 2, pt. 2, eds. Michael W. Jennings, Howard Eiland, and Gary Smith (Cambridge, Mass. and London, England: The Belknap Press of Harvard University Press, 1999), 768–782.

Fernand Léger

ARGENTAN, 1881 — GIF-SUR-YVETTE, 1955

1

Smoke over the Rooftops, 1912

Oil on paper, 25 1/4 x 19 5/8 in. (64.3 x 50 cm.)

Private Collection

Photograph © R. Lorenzson

All dimensions are height x width

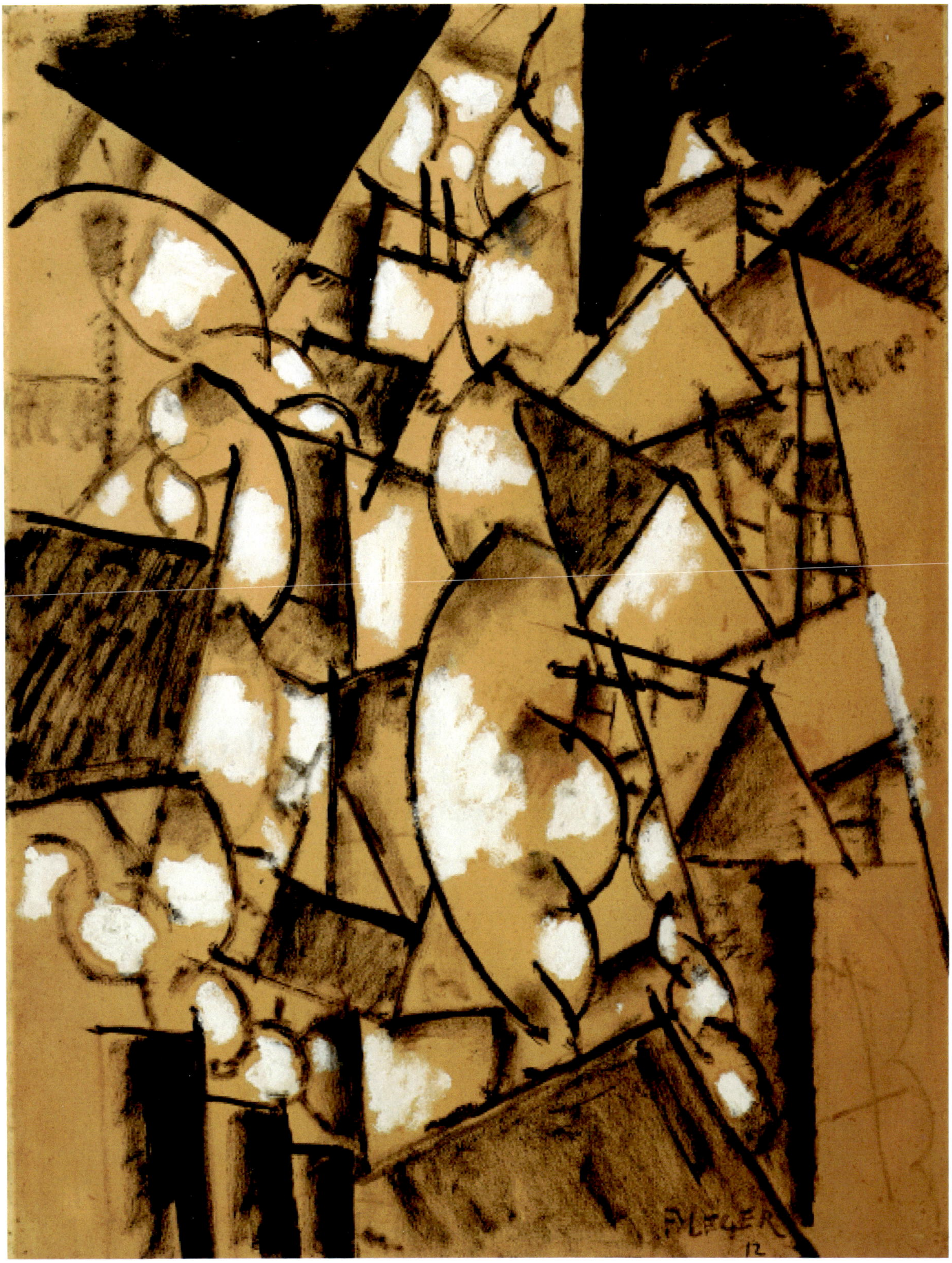
F. LEGER
12

2

Study for "Nude Model in the Studio"/
Composition 1, 1912
Oil and gouache on paper, 25¼ x 19 in. (64.1 x 48.3 cm.)
Courtesy of The Metropolitan Museum of Art,
Lent by the Alex Hillman Family Foundation (L.1988.92.9).
Photograph ©2006 The Metropolitan Museum of Art

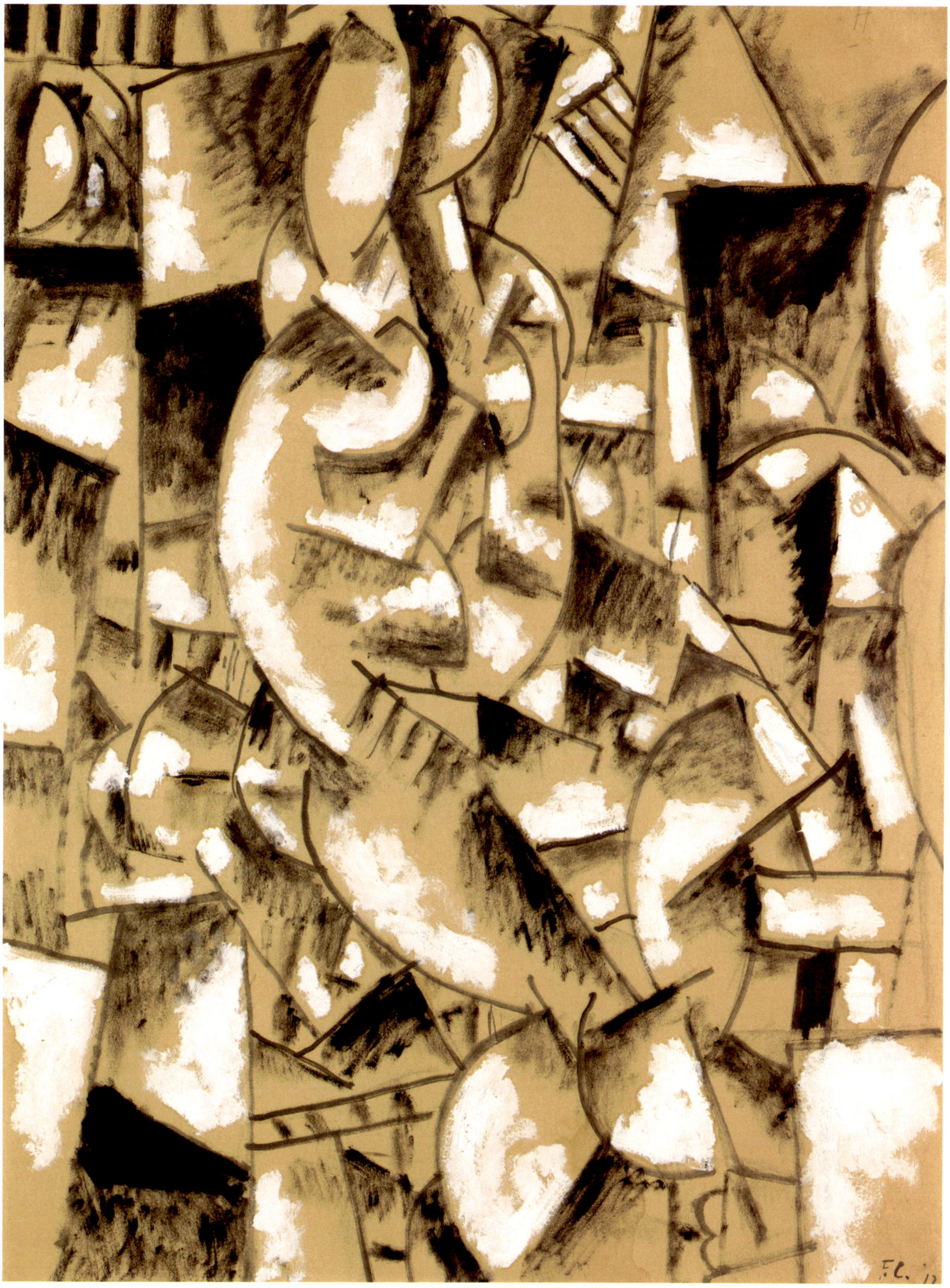

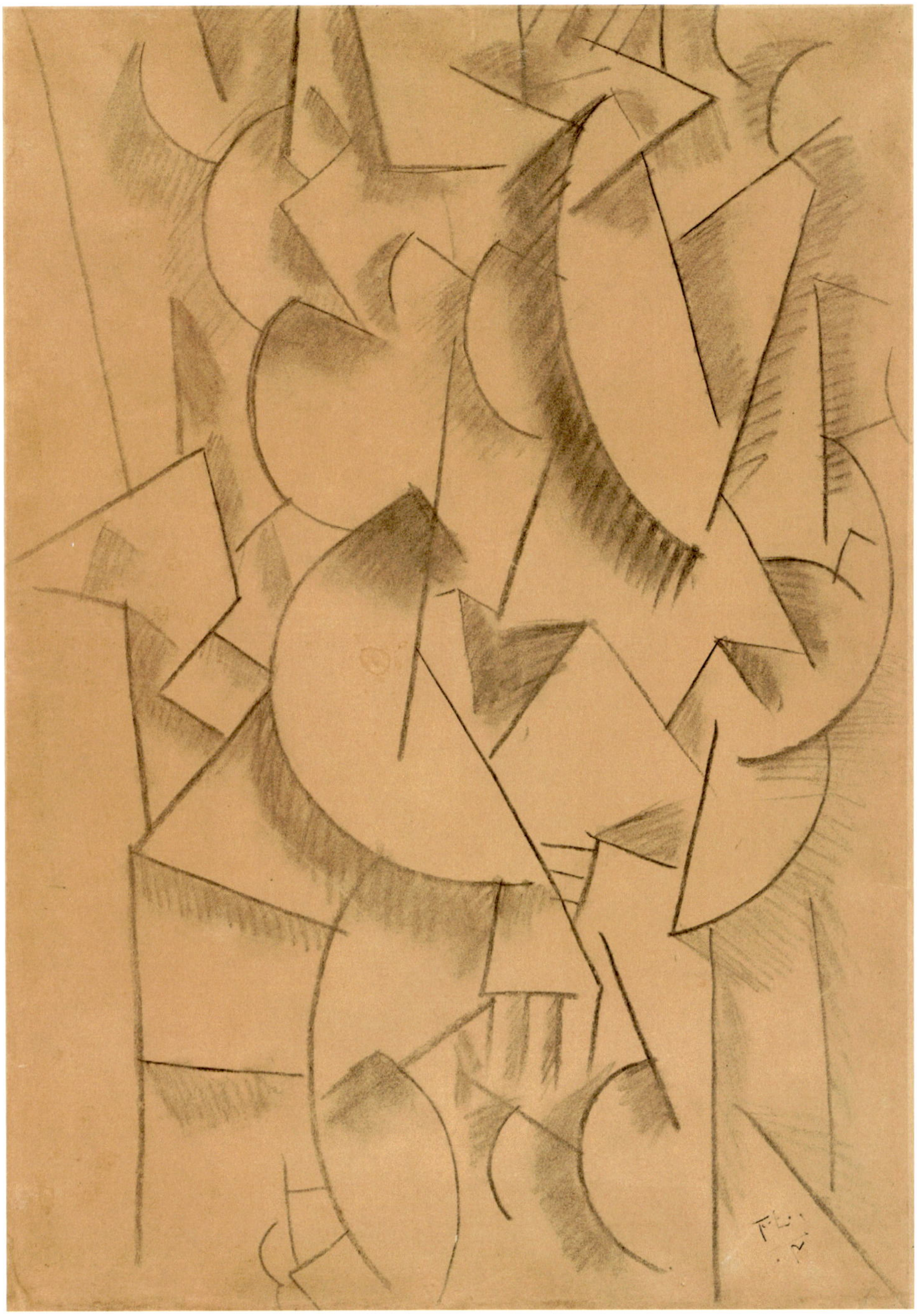

3a

Contrast of Forms, 1912

Charcoal on paper, 25¼ x 18 in. (64.1 x 45.7 cm.) (recto)

Gift of Jo Carole and Ronald S. Lauder (119.1986.a)

The Museum of Modern Art, New York

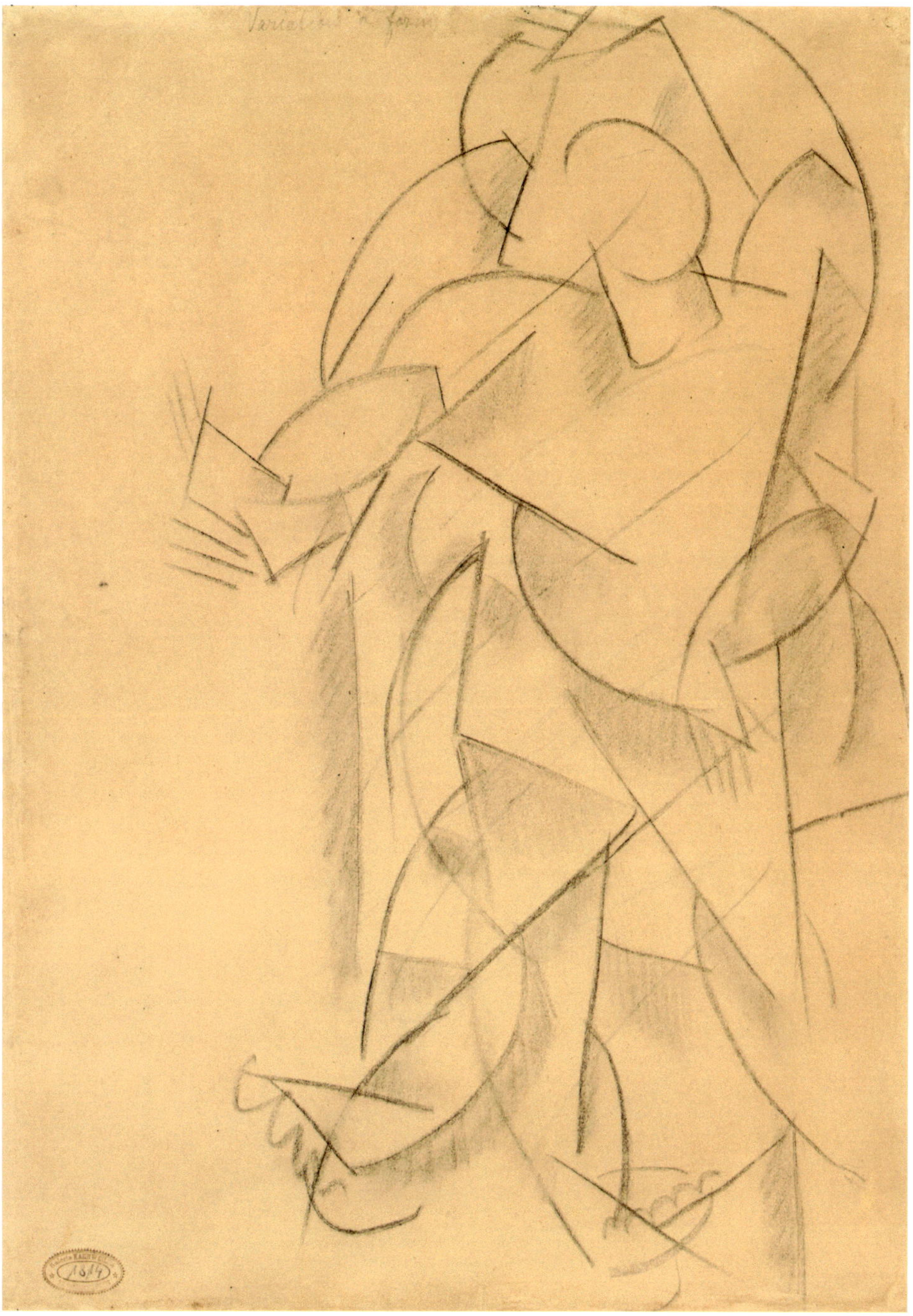

3b

Contrast of Forms, 1912

Charcoal on paper, 25¼ x 18 in. (64.1 x 45.7 cm.) (verso)

Gift of Jo Carole and Ronald S. Lauder (119.1986.b)

The Museum of Modern Art, New York

4

Composition (Contrast of Forms), 1912–13
Gouache, brush, and India ink on buff paper,
mounted on board, $23\frac{1}{2}$ x 20 in. (59.6 x 50.8 cm.)
Collection Michael and Judy Steinhardt, New York

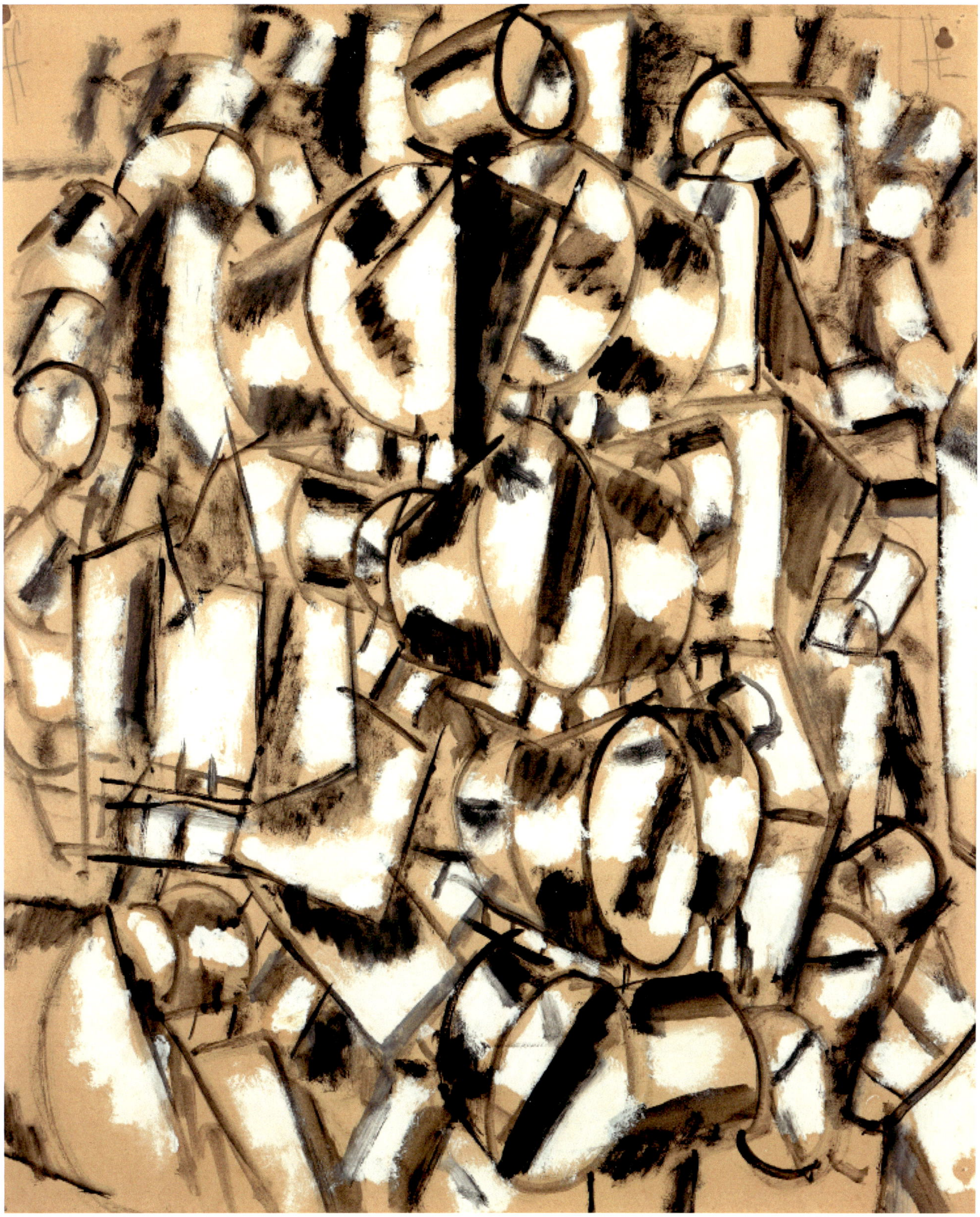

5

Two Reclining Women, 1913

Gouache and charcoal on paper, 19¾ x 25½ in. (50.2 x 64.8 cm.)

The Metropolitan Museum of Art, Gift of

Mr. and Mrs. William R. Acquavella, 1986 (1986.396.1).

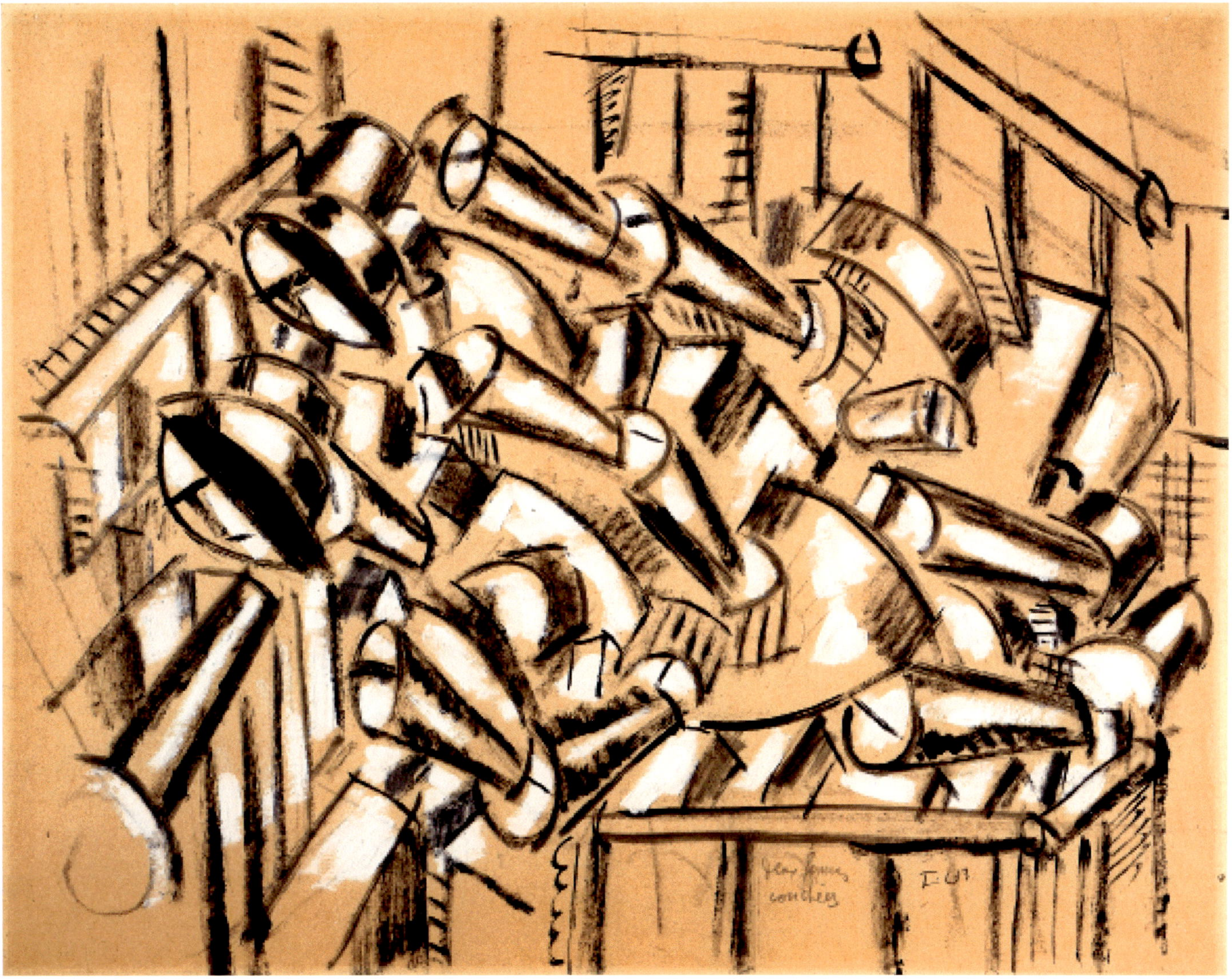

6

Study for "Contrast of Forms," 1913

Gouache on paper, mounted on cardboard, 19½ x 24 in. (49.6 x 61.2 cm.)

Solomon R. Guggenheim Museum, New York

48.1172.50

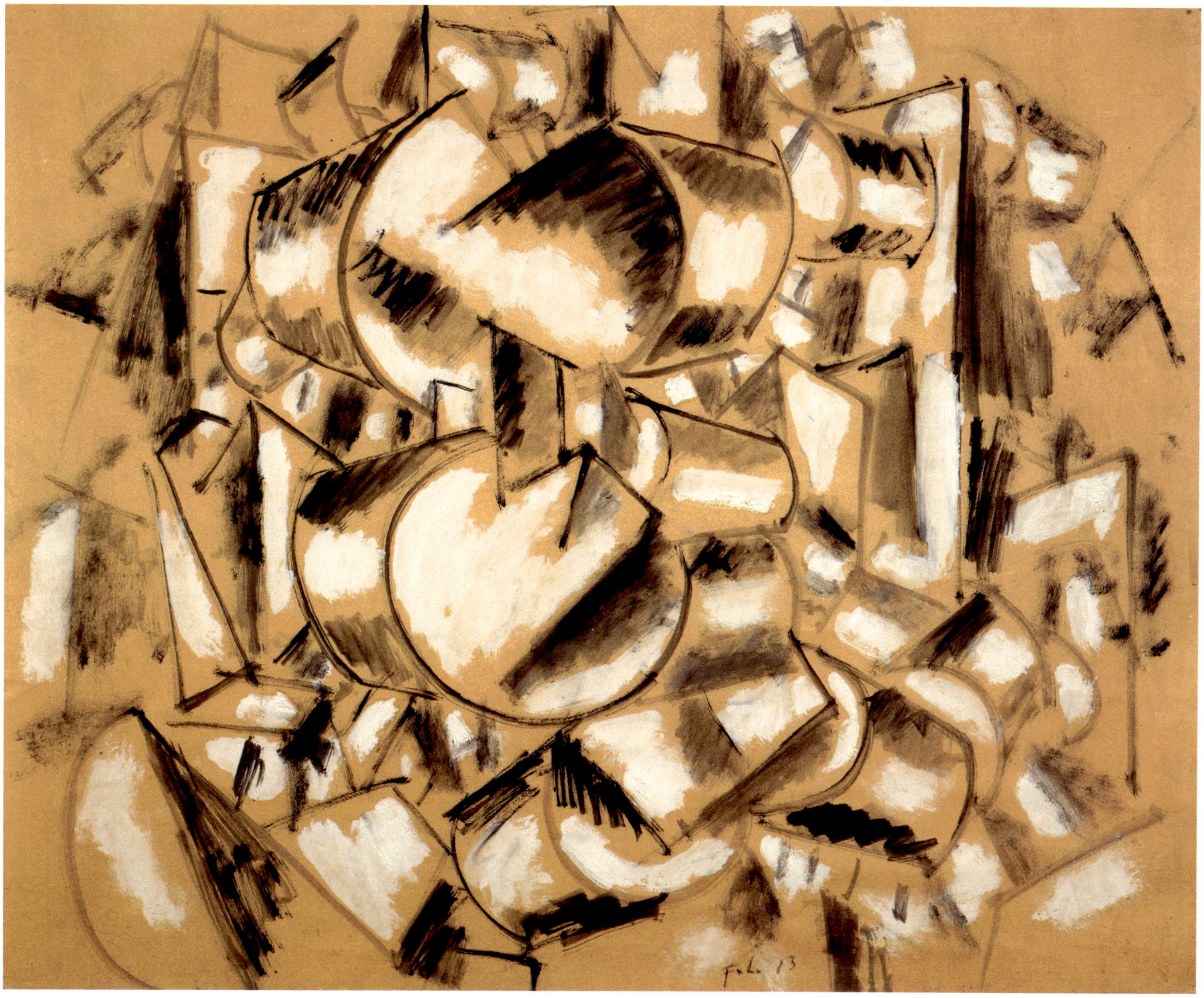

7

Contrast of Forms, 1913

India ink, wash, and gouache on buff paper, $16\frac{3}{8}$ x $19\frac{1}{4}$ in. (41.5 x 49 cm.)

Private Collection

Photograph © R. Lorenzson

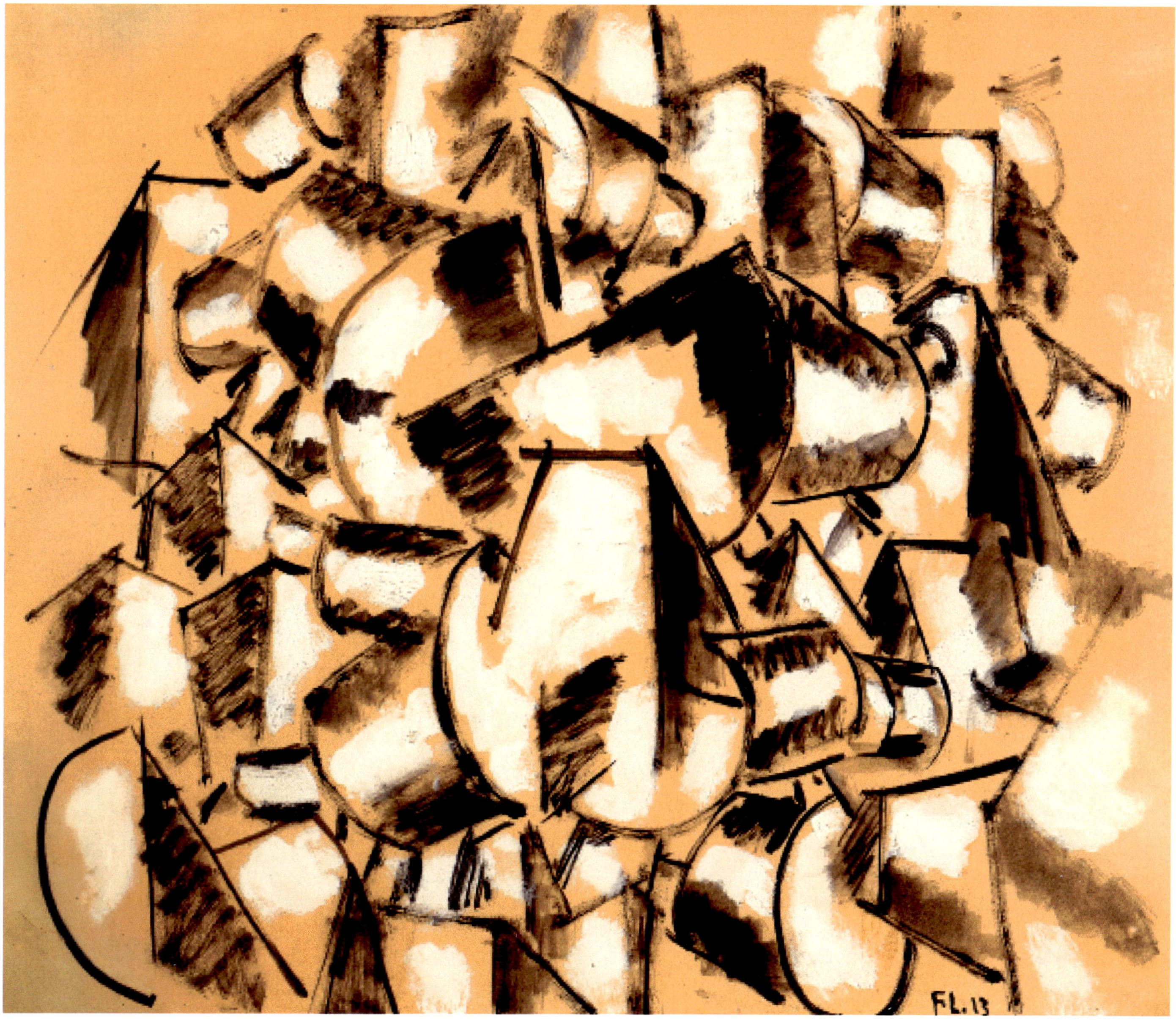
F.L. 13

8

Study for "Still Life," 1913

Gouache and oil on paper, 18¾ x 23¼ in. (47.7 x 59.3 cm.)

Private Collection

Photograph © Dorothy Zeidman

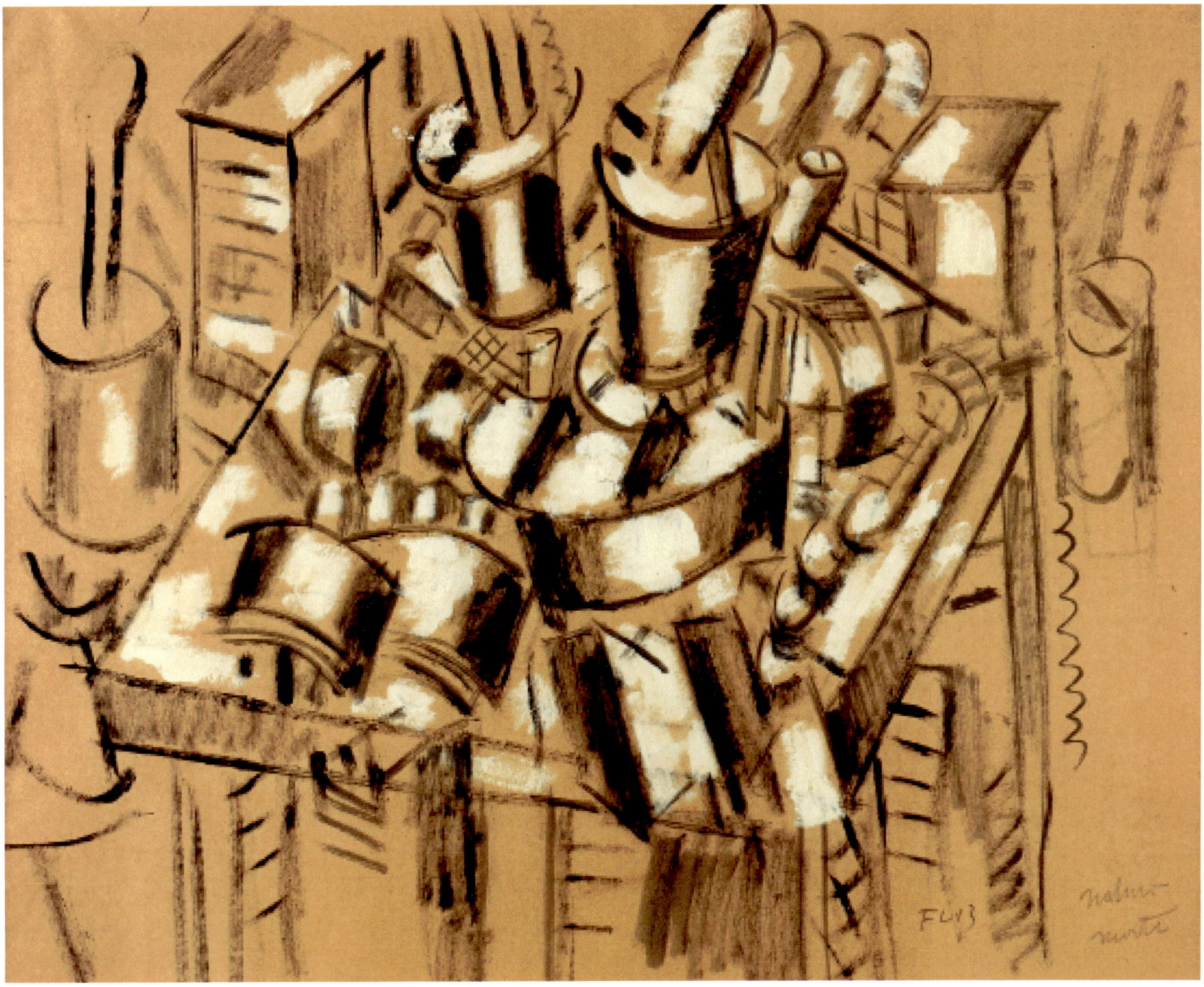

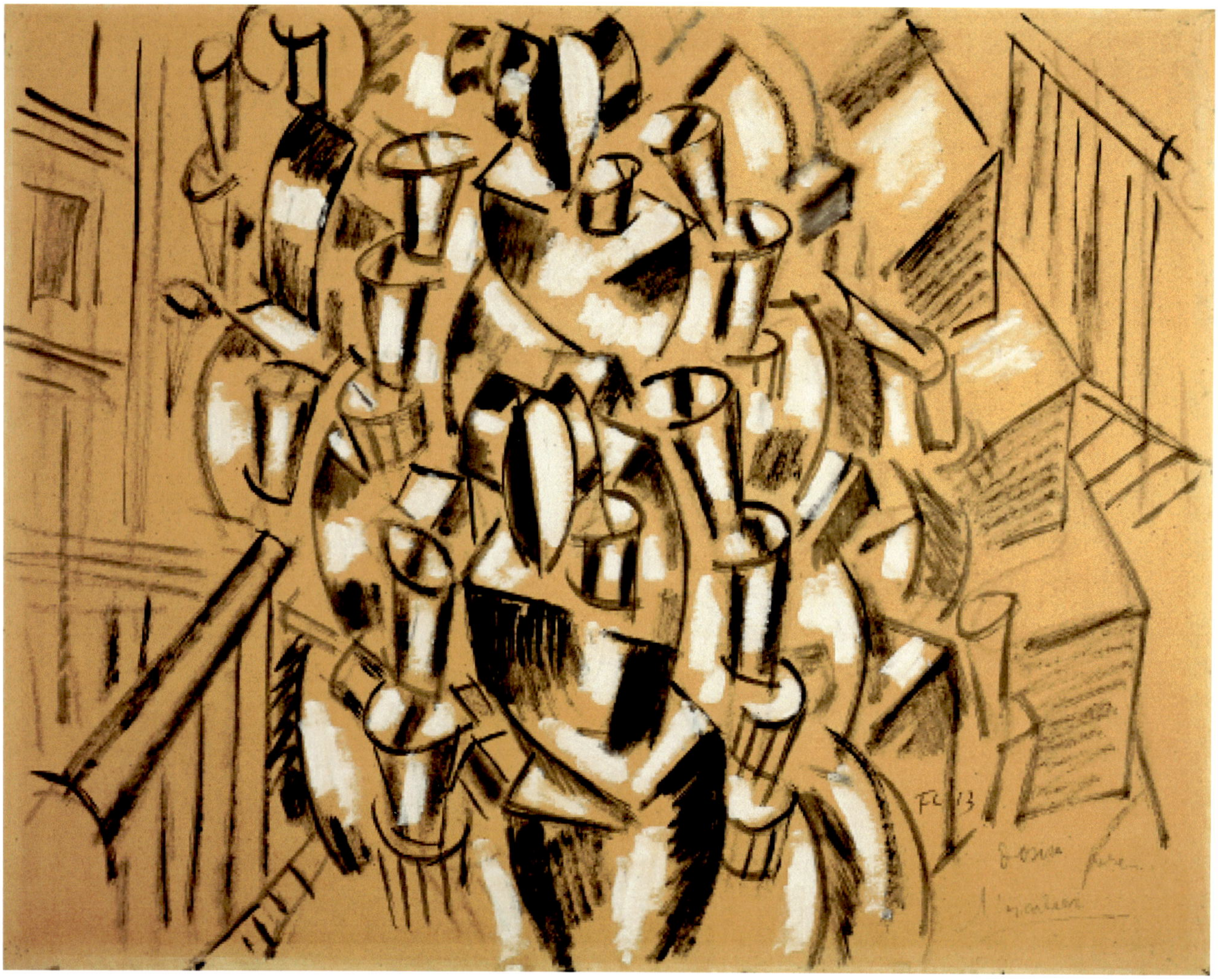

9

Study for "The Staircase," 1913

Gouache and India ink on buff paper, 19⅝ x 25⅝ in. (50 x 65 cm.)

Private Collection

Photograph © R. Lorenzson

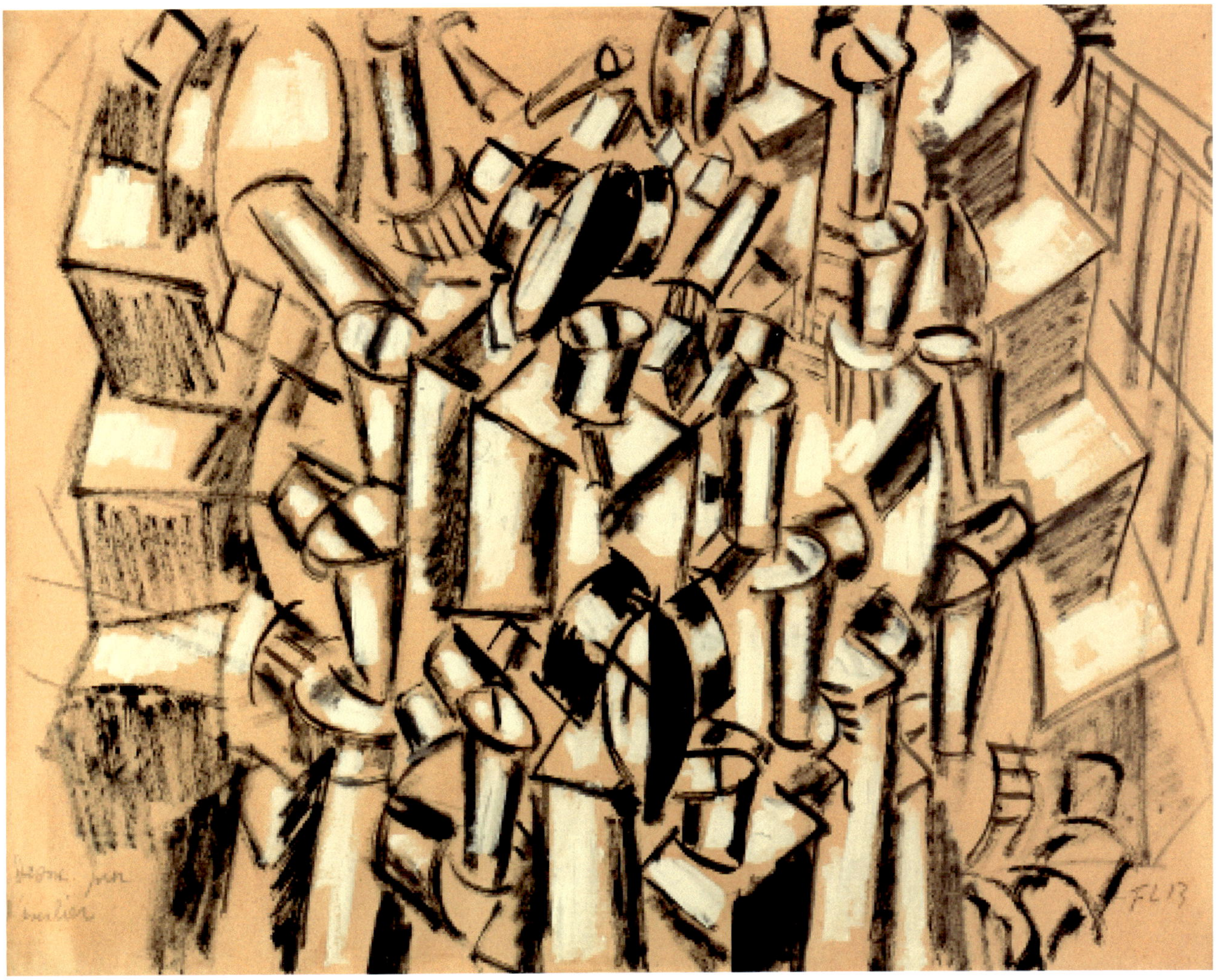

10

Study for "The Staircase," 1913

Gouache and ink on paper, 19 x 25 in. (48.2 x 63.5 cm.)

Private Collection

Photograph © Dorothy Zeidman

11

Study for the Painting "Still Life with an Alarm Clock," 1914

Gouache and charcoal on paper, 25½ x19⅜ in. (64.8 x 49.2 cm.)

The Metropolitan Museum of Art,

Gift of Mr. and Mrs. William R. Acquavella, 1986 (1986.396.2).

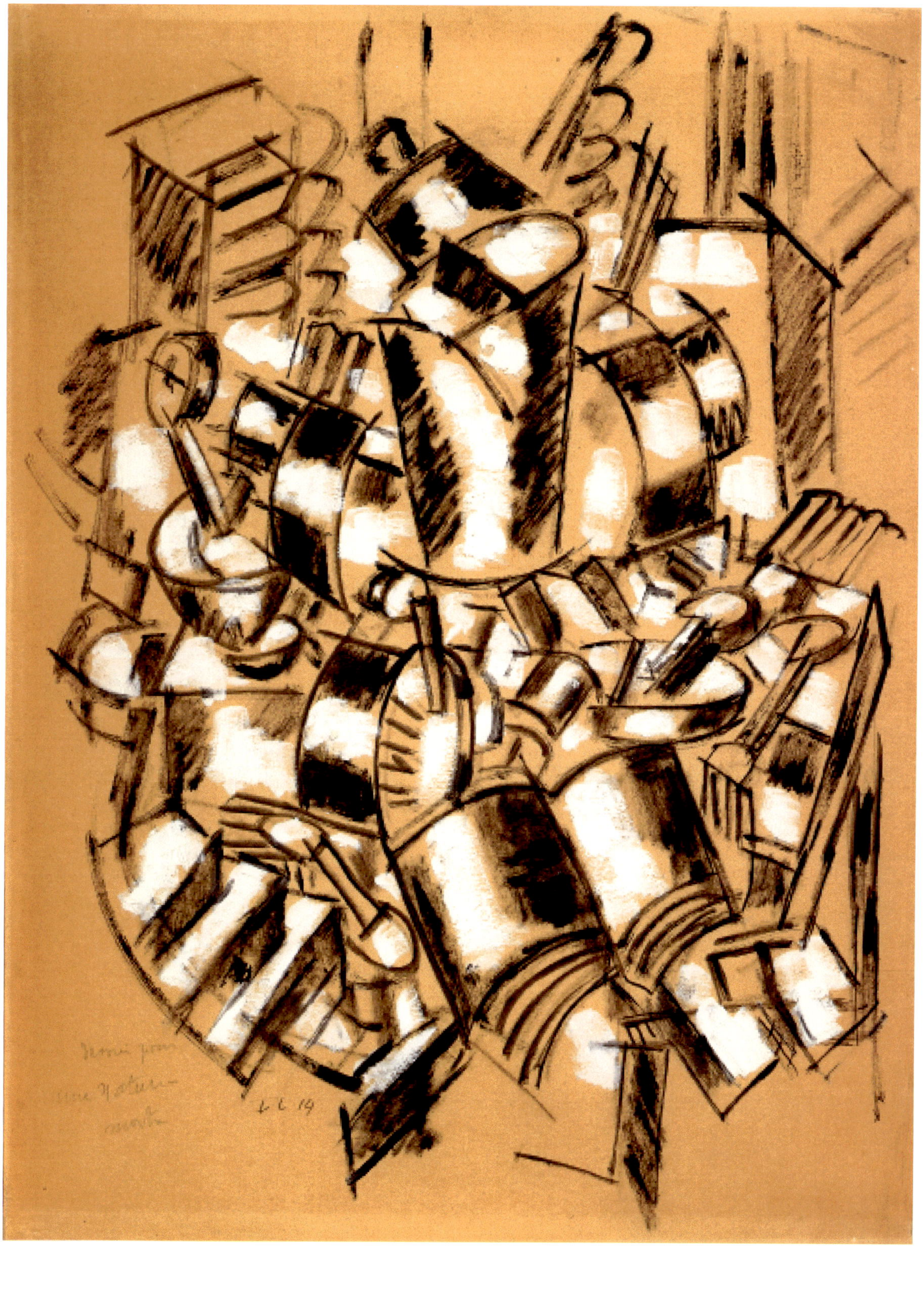

12

Village in the Forest, 1914

Oil on burlap, 29 1/8 x 36 5/8 in. (73.97 x 93.02 cm.)

Collection Albright-Knox Art Gallery, Buffalo, New York

Gift of A. Conger Goodyear, 1960

1960:4

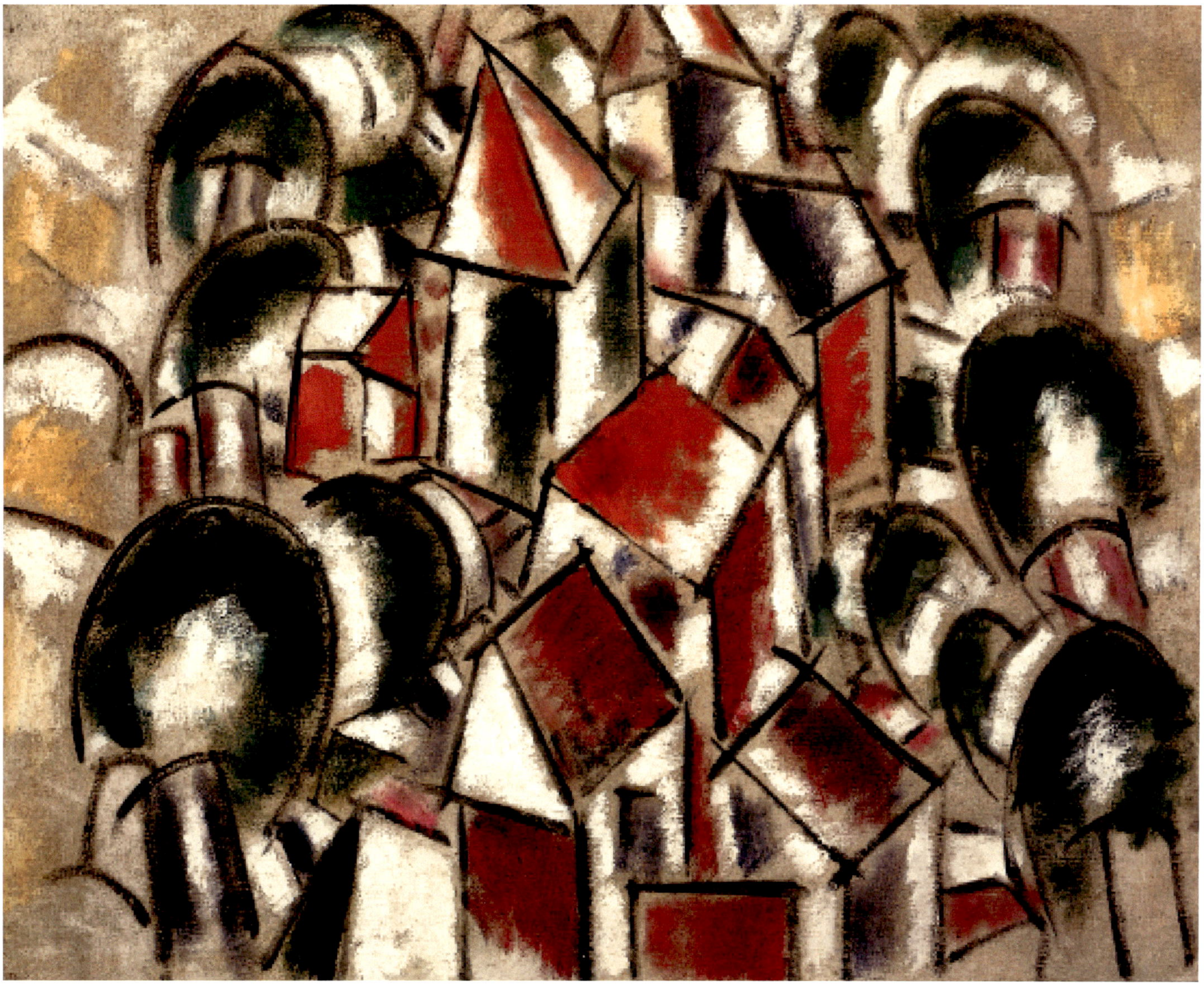

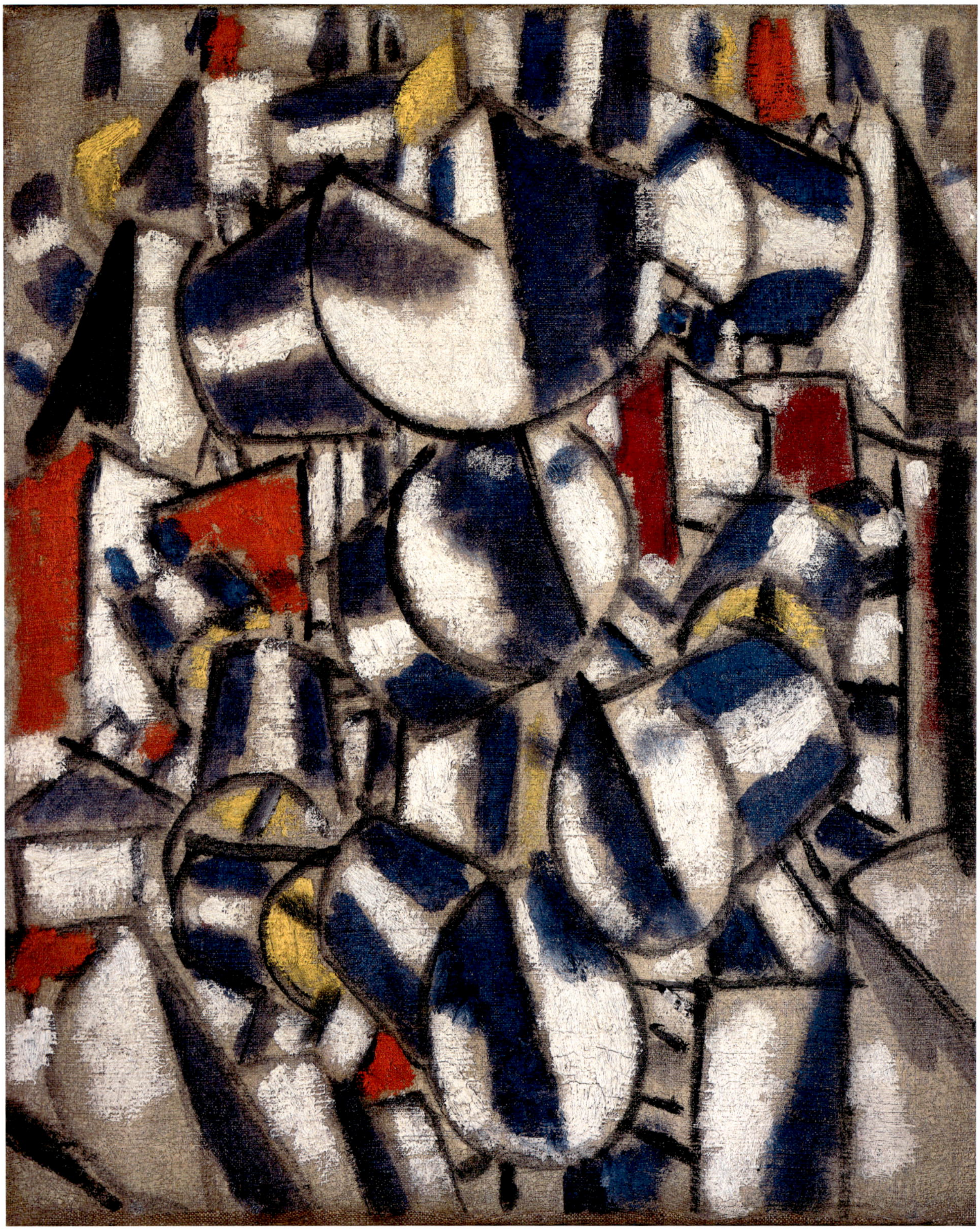

13

Contrast of Forms, 1913

Oil on canvas, 21 5/8 x 18 1/8 in. (55x46 cm.)

Private Collection

Photograph © Ellen Page Wilson / PaceWildenstein